The
Partakers

The
Partakers
Holy Spirit Power
for Persevering Christians

Robert G. Tuttle, Jr.

ABINGDON PRESS
Nashville   New York

THE PARTAKERS

Copyright © 1974 by Abingdon Press

Library of Congress Cataloging in Publication Data

Tuttle, Robert G   1941-
  The partakers.

  Includes bibliographical references.
  1. Holy Spirit.   I. Title.
BT121.2.T87   234'.1   74-9561
ISBN 0-687-30109-2

MANUFACTURED BY THE PARTHENON PRESS AT
NASHVILLE, TENNESSEE, UNITED STATES OF AMERICA

■ **To Pati**

Acknowledgments

Don Bacon, for endless hours of typing and whose witness for Jesus Christ is an absolute inspiration.

Larry Lacour, the staff and members of the First United Methodist Church of Colorado Springs, for providing the platform where I first put *The Partakers* to the test.

Contents

Preface

Martin Luther was once asked if Thomas Munzer, a young enthusiast, had the Holy Spirit. "Yes," Luther replied, "Munzer has the Holy Spirit; he has eaten him, feathers and all." Many so-called Spirit-filled Christians seem to have "eaten him, feathers and all." This book, however, is written with the conviction that one can receive all that God has to offer and still have *balance,* still be a *real person.*

We live in a world that is seeking power—power to cope, power to propel us beyond the level of mere existence, power to overcome life's problems, power to live life at peak, power to rise to the surface, power to teach these whirlwinds we live in how to dance. A nation seeks power to overcome the threat of a democracy gone wrong, scandal, inflation, the drain of war. A community seeks power to overcome the pressures of a mobile society, racial prejudice, drug abuse. An individual seeks power to reshape, to remold, to re-create. Jesus bequeaths us such power, magnificent power, power to raise the dead, to heal the sick, to overcome and to endure. That power is the Holy Spirit. Over three hundred times in the New Testament the Holy Spirit is associated with power. You and I, therefore, have not scratched the surface with regard to what is available to us through faith in Jesus Christ and the power of his Spirit. Yet, some of us don't believe in that power.

Not too long ago I was talking to a man in prison. Suddenly he shouted through the bars, "Preacher, God can't change me!" I replied, "Sir, how long have you been an atheist?" He responded immediately, "I'm not an atheist, I believe in God"; to which I again replied, "Friend, if your god can't change you, you don't have a god. What good is a god who can't make a difference?" A god without power is no god; but let's face it, many of us feel this way, at least at times.

We do have a powerful God who can and will change us if we yield to him. Yet many of us are afraid of such power.

I honestly believe that it will be easier for me to die than it was for me to become a Christian. I was afraid of the yes with a divine catch; "the 'yes' that entails other 'yeses'."[1] I recently had lunch with a man who kept emphasizing how God's gift is free, and then, being reminded of my initial struggle with God, I added, "True, but if you accept the gift, you belong to the

[1] Michel Quoist, *Prayers* (New York: Sheed & Ward, 1963), p. 121.

Giver.'' The Giver—he was my problem. I was certain that he was some kind of benign killjoy. It never occurred to me that all God wanted for my life was that I should get everything good in life that is so much a part of abundant living. I had no cause to fear such power. The Holy Spirit wouldn't embarrass me; I wouldn't have to appear strange or self-righteous. After all, my being a Christian doesn't make me better than *someone else,* it makes me better than what *I* was. Furthermore, God didn't wish to put me into a box. I could still be responsibly free. In fact, I could receive not only his gift of salvation, but all his good gifts and still be genuinely me.

This book, therefore, will be *theological* insofar as I believe that Christians have a right to know that there are good reasons for believing as they do. Too much Christianity (especially that which seeks to interpret the work of the Holy Spirit) has been long on experience and short on theology. Many popular books on the Holy Spirit are not teaching bad theology, they just aren't teaching enough good theology to keep people from hearing the wrong kinds of things. Let me illustrate. If I were to use the phrase ''the Baptism of the Holy Spirit'' without defining it carefully, most of you would be hearing ''speaking in tongues.'' Without jumping too far ahead of myself simply let me say that this is *not* scriptural Christianity.

This book will be *evangelical* in that I believe that relationship with God is *initiated* only through faith in Jesus Christ. Every time I see the sign ''Get right with God,'' I practically go into shock. One doesn't get right with God, one is *put* right with God. God alone plays the principal role in the drama of rescue. I John 4:19 reads, "We love, because he first loved us." [2]

This book will be *charismatic* insofar as I believe that the Holy Spirit is the stuff of which music is made. I believe that the same power that was available to Jesus is also available to us. I look out of my window now at Pike's Peak shooting up over fourteen thousand feet out of the plains of Colorado. Imagine the power that could command such a mountain to be moved!

This book will be vitally concerned with what has been commonly called *social action*. Good news concerns reconciliation wherever separation has occurred. We live in a world of gaps. The enemy, a negative life force that seeks to separate us from God and from one another, manifests himself on many different fronts. There are racial gaps, cultural gaps, affluency gaps, intellectual gaps, generation gaps, ecology gaps, and many, many others. Evangelical charismatic Christians, therefore, had better be providing avenue upon avenue for the faith to manifest itself in the service of reconciliation throughout the community, lest this faith not be worth the blood of an old goat, let alone the blood of Jesus Christ.

This book will be *personal* insofar as I believe that one speaks most effectively out of his own experience. In a very real sense, this book is me, "warts and all."

This book, therefore, is written for those of us who

---

[2] *Today's English Version* translates the Greek word *dikaios* correctly as "put right with." See Rom. 2:13.

need first of all to recognize God's power. Then it is for those of us who need to know how to plug into that power boldly, yet with balance. Most of all, however, it is for those of us who want more than anything else to move in the power of the Holy Spirit toward full maturity. So, why "the partakers"? The Greek word *summetokos* (translated the "partakers"or those who "share with") was coined for the New Testament and never appears in the Old Testament or in secular writings. It is used only in reference to the power and promise of the Holy Spirit. It is consummated only *after* the faithful endurance of the believer. Capturing the spirit of this word, therefore, this book is not for some "super-saint," but for those of us who by the power of the Holy Spirit want not only to begin but to "run with perseverance the race that is set before us" to fight the good fight, to keep the faith, to become in fact the partakers.

For it is impossible to restore again to repentance those who have once been enlightened, who have tasted the heavenly gift, and have become partakers of the Holy Spirit, and have tasted the goodness of the word of God and the powers of the age to come, if they then commit apostasy, since they crucify the Son of God on their own account and hold him up to contempt. For land which has drunk the rain that often falls upon it, and brings forth vegetation useful to those for whose sake it is cultivated, receives a blessing from God. But if it bears thorns and thistles, it is worthless and near to being cursed; its end is to be burned. (Hebrews 6:4-8)

PART I

The Holy Spirit in the Life of the Believer

Chapter I
The Life of God in the Soul of Man

Too many books dealing with the charismatic movement are noticeably lacking in any real attempt to articulate intelligently a theology of the Holy Spirit. Chapters 1 and 2, therefore, focus on such a theology accented by my own personal experience.

Unfortunately when it comes to describing the work of the Holy Spirit, many neo-Pentecostal churches (mainline denominational churches now identifying with the charismatic movement) accept the charismatic movement at the point of its greatest weakness (its theology), which undermines its greatest strength (its power and enthusiasm). I have a Presbyterian minister friend, for example, who is no longer identifiable as a Presbyterian and consequently can now minister to Pentecostals, who don't need him, and cannot minister to Presbyterians, who do. This chapter is an attempt to interpret the power and enthusiasm of the charismatic movement in light of my own experience and tradition, not that this is the only way to interpret the movement or even the best way. Just as the Presbyterian would begin with the sovereignty of God, and the Roman Catholic with the Sacraments, I begin with John Wesley's theology of grace, because this is the handle that I know best.[1]

Prior to John Wesley's evangelical conversion he was much impressed by the works of a Scotsman, a mystic named Henry Scougal. Scougal's book *The Life of God in the Soul of Man* was a classic among those of the eighteenth century who were in dead earnest about what it meant to be God's person. Wesley, taking Scougal's lead, frequently referred to the phrase "the life of God in the soul of man" when talking about the work of the Holy Spirit. Wesley speaks of the Holy Spirit in terms of grace (Holy Spirit and grace are synonymous in all of Wesley's writing), more specifically, *prevenient, justifying, and sanctifying* grace.

Prevenient, or preventing, grace refers to the work of the Holy Spirit in the life of the believer almost from the moment of conception until the child of God accepts for himself or herself Jesus Christ personally. The Holy Spirit *prevents* the child, usually through the nurture of Christian parents or friends, from wandering too far from

[1] For those who would like to study the charismatic movement interpreted another way, see the *Report of the Special Committee on the Work of the Holy Spirit* to the 182nd General Assembly of the United Presbyterian Church in the U.S.A., 1970, or Kevin and Dorothy Ranaghan, *Catholic Pentecostals* (Paramus, N.J.: Paulist Press, 1969).

the way. This same Holy Spirit ensures for the child upon reaching the age of reason, freedom to choose. Good theology, though often neglected, teaches us that without this selfsame Spirit there would be no freedom to decide. We would all "choose" to remain in sin, never claiming our "election" in Jesus Christ if the Holy Spirit were not already at work in our lives. Let me illustrate this with a true story.

I once led a man who was in prison to Christ. He had spent twenty-five out of forty-four years behind bars. One night I went to visit him, and as I came to his cell he said to me, "Bob, I laid awake last night thinking and suddenly it dawned on me that it takes an average of twenty-five different witnesses before any real encounter with God takes place. I want you to know that just because you were number twenty-five you think you did it all and you stink." Wham! He got me! He forced me to admit—that's the problem with us evangelicals. Just because we're number twenty-five we think we did it all, when twenty-four just as important have gone before us. The influence of those used in prevenient grace is vitally important—the one to twenty-four. Although my parents were not able to call forth in me full response to the gospel, I would be the most ungrateful wretch in the whole world if I did not say now that I am a Christian today because of them. It is tragic that many evangelicals fail to sense affirmation or satisfaction in being one to twenty-four—or in being twenty-six to fifty, for that matter, when all are *vitally* important.

Prevenient grace suggests that the Holy Spirit gently

woos us, ever drawing us to the Father. He reveals the very nature of the Father's love. I remember before my last year in college I had been working the wheat harvest in the Far West with a friend. On our way back East we decided to make a brief stop at the Grand Canyon. I shall never forget walking out on the rim of the canyon and seeing not only a lovely view but a lovely girl as well. She had on a college sweatshirt, and since I was a bit impetuous I remember thinking out loud to myself (making sure that she could hear me) where that particular college was located. A brief reply thrown rather casually over her shoulder was all the introduction I needed, and in a half hour's time she knew my life's history. It was clear to her that I was not a Christian. Much to my surprise, I remember, she began to share with me ever so carefully fresh insight into the Christian faith. Touching on all the essentials of repentance and faith in Christ she wove those gospel bones into the flesh of her own experience. I have frequently said that her witness was so much a part of her living that I could not tell where one left off and the other began. Quite simply, she slipped up on me; the Holy Spirit was gently tugging. In a very quiet, unassuming way, she began by telling me that God loved me like a father. Unlike many, this was not difficult for me to understand, since my own father loved me and I knew it. I knew that he and my mother both loved me the way no one else could ever love me because I was a part of them. It's natural to love that which is a part of us. It was then that I realized that I was as much a part of God as I was a part of my parents, and God loved me the way my own parents loved me *times infinity*. That's some kind of love! I was soon to learn that that kind of love can be trusted.

I remember returning to college with the demands of the gospel full upon my mind. I gradually began to realize that life has to be more important than just making a living, "bringing home the bacon." I remember adding up all the things that were most important to me —finishing law school, getting established in practice, getting established in the community, getting married, raising children, building a home, all those wonderfully important things that most people count as happiness. Suddenly, however, I realized that the only common denominator in all those things was me. I'll let you in on a little secret. A man with himself as the only common denominator in life lives in a mighty small world, and I got bored and I got scared. I remember late one night at the foot of my bed on the top floor of the fraternity house praying, "God, if there is a God [and I wasn't really sure], Christ, if there is a Christ [and I was even less sure of that], I give my whole life to you." Now admittedly that doesn't sound like faith, but don't knock it, because I haven't been the same since. My life was changed. The gentle tug of the Holy Spirit has enabled me to say "yes" to God.

This brings us to justifying grace. The "yes" to God means that the Holy Spirit no longer gently tugs but now flushes us, cleansing us from all sin. This is the essence of New Testament Christianity. The New Testament or new covenant no longer covers over sin (propitiation) as in the old covenant under the law, but roots out sin (expiation) through faith in Jesus Christ. Theologians talk about *imputed* righteousness, which simply means that the *righteousness of Jesus Christ* has now been *attributed to us through faith in him*. God sees us no longer through our own righteousness but through the righteousness that was in Jesus Christ. The Holy Spirit, however, does not stop here. From the moment of justification or having been put right with God, sanctifying grace then begins moving us toward *imparted* righteousness or the *righteousness of Jesus Christ* not simply attributed to us through faith in him but now *realized in us*.[2] The Christian faith is an adventure or journey between imputed and imparted righteousness. Truly, we are being saved. Wesley called this process "the search for the renewal of the soul in the image of God." In fact, until the righteousness of Jesus Christ, which has been attributed to us through faith in him, has become realized in us, we are not "ripe for glory." Sanctifying grace, therefore, is the work of the Spirit that makes us holy. The Spirit is called holy as a description not of his nature (the Father and Son are also holy), but of his function

[2] *Imputed righteousness:* Imagine standing as the defendant before a judge in a court of law. You are guilty. Several witnesses saw the crime committed. The judge suddenly summons his own son to stand beside you. He says in effect: "I love you so much I give you my son's innocence and I give your sin to my son who will pay the price—death! Case against the defendant dismissed." *Imparted righteousness:* Imagine the same court of law, ten, twenty, thirty years later. Again, you stand before the judge. This time, however, as a result of your own ensuing righteousness you and the son are now so closely identified that you stand as one and the judge again pronounces, "Case dismissed!"

—the Spirit who makes us holy. Now we begin to understand the Hebrews' call to "the holiness without which no one will see the Lord" (Hebrews 12:14).

If imputed righteousness is not moving toward imparted righteousness we are simply not practicing what we preach. John Wesley makes this point crystal clear in a well-known quotation: "The doctrines of justification and salvation by faith are grievously abused by many Methodists. I find more profit in sermons on either good tempers or good works than in what are vulgarly called gospel sermons. That term is now become a mere *cant* word. I wish none of our society would use it. It has no determinate meaning. Let but a pert, self-sufficient animal, that has neither sense nor grace, bawl out something about Christ and his blood or justification by faith, and all his hearers cry out, 'What a fine gospel sermon!' Surely the Methodists have not so learnt Christ. We know no gospel without salvation from sin."[3] How's that for a shot at "cheap grace"? And we thought that Bonhoeffer said it first. Again, good theology teaches us to fear and abhor sin far more than death or hell. William Hordern seems to feel that much of the new interest in sanctification can be found among those who feel barely saved from hell but not from sin. In Barth's *Dogmatics* we find: "What is the forgiveness of sins if it is not directly accompanied by an actual liberation from the commital of sin? . . . What is faith without

---

[3] John Wesley, *Works,* ed. Thomas Jackson, 3rd ed. (Grand Rapids: Zondervan, 1959), XIII, 36.

25

obedience?"[4] Another quotation from John Wesley states that salvation is "a present deliverance from sin; a restoration of the soul to its primitive health, its original purity; a recovery of the divine nature; the renewal of our souls after the image of God."[5] Sanctifying grace along with the fruit and the gifts of the Holy Spirit has been provided by God to assist us in moving from imputed to imparted righteousness. "The righteousness of Christ is doubtless necessary for any soul that enters into glory: But so is personal holiness too, for every child of man. . . . The former is necessary to *entitle* us to heaven; the latter to *qualify* us for it."[6]

So, the Holy Spirit from the time of our conception gently tugs until at last our "yes" enables the Holy Spirit to cleanse and indwell as we accept for ourselves the righteousness of Jesus Christ. This is not the end, however. In fact, this is only the beginning. For those who understand and can accept the Wesleyan tradition, Christianity, the whole of it, from the moment of justification, is an adventure between the righteousness of Christ attributed to us and the righteousness of Christ realized in us—the goal of the Spirit-filled life. Although Wesley arrived at this doctrine prior to his own evangelical conversion it lay dormant until the Revival began producing Christians who then fell away from the faith unless they

[4] Karl Barth, *Church Dogmatics*, ed. G. W. Bromiley and T. F. Torrance (Edinburgh: T. & T. Clark, 1958), Vol. IV, Pt. 2, p. 505.

[5] Southey, *The Life of Wesley* (London: Longman, 1858), II, 301.2.

[6] John Wesley, *Works*, ed. Thomas Jackson (London: Wesleyan Conference Office, 3rd ed., 1872), VII, 314.

continued to grow.[7] Wesley, therefore, was concerned to retrieve backsliding Christians. In order to make sturdy warriors out of mere struggling Christians, he enforced this doctrine of perpetual growth through sanctifying grace. Perfection or holiness was considered the goal of the Spirit-filled life. Again, this goal was not a static but a dynamic one, always improvable, but it became more and more for Wesley the "one purpose of religion."

For the partaker, therefore, prideful self-righteousness cannot be a part of the Spirit-filled life, since sanctification, though attainable, is never completed. Spirit-filled Christians give all that they know of themselves to all that they know of God. This means that each day they find out more and more about themselves and consequently have more of themselves to give to God. Simi-

[7] For those interested in how Wesley arrived at this doctrine, much of it came from the influence of some rather obscure Roman Catholic mystics. Very briefly, there are five stages in classical mysticism: awakening (a moral or ethical awakening), purgation (in which one suppresses the flesh so that it no longer interferes with the Spirit), illumination (in which God sends "shafts of light" into the soul or "sensible comforts" so that the mystic has just for a moment an awareness of God's presence), the dark night of the soul (in which God withdraws these comforts, forcing the mystic to come by naked faith or blind trust), and union with God (in which the mystic becomes one with God). Wesley, although eventually disillusioned with the dark night of the soul (Faith as blind trust soon lost its appeal), continued to teach the first three stages, substituted the Reformation doctrine of faith as the "assurance of things hoped for, the conviction of things not seen" for the dark night of the soul, and let that carry him through to union with God which he called perfection. To ensure perpetual growth beyond the fifth stage or union with God, Wesley defined this perfection as subjective and relative, not angelic, Adamic, or absolute.

27

larly, each day they find out more and more about God so that they have more God to commit themselves to. This perpetual growth by the power of the Holy Spirit is the particular genius of this interpretation of the life of God in the soul of man.   10/6/74

Chapter II
To the Father, Through the Son, by the Holy Spirit

If Karl Barth is correct in assuming that theology is "faith seeking understanding" it is now time to interpret the tradition and experience of chapter 1 within the context of a triune God. How many times have I been asked, "What is the difference between Father, Son, and Holy Spirit? To whom do I pray? What does it mean, a triune God?" God is Father, Son, and Holy Spirit. This is not only the traditional teaching of the church, this is the essence of Christian experience. I have already suggested that several years ago I was led to God the Father, through God the Son, by God the Holy Spirit.

What does it mean, God has three persons? Theological journals have been struggling with theories for close to two thousand years, yet none is fully satisfying. After all, I am told that heresy is born when little minds try to solve big paradoxes. Very briefly, there is a simple little analogy, which is not at all original, let alone satisfying, but which might possibly prove helpful. Water can be either frozen or boiled and still have basically two parts of hydrogen and one part of oxygen whether it is ice or steam.[1]

The expression "God has three persons" can be misleading. The word "person" comes from *persona,* the mask worn in Greek and Roman theater denoting role or function, not separate person. God is indeed one God who functions as Father, Son, and Holy Spirit; God the Father—Creator; God the Son—Redeemer; God the Holy Spirit—Creator—Redeemer within us or, more simply, God the Father for us, God the Son with us, and God the Holy Spirit within us.[2]

I sometimes lose patience with so many who are in actuality Unitarian (those who deny the trinity by isolating God the Father) without knowing it. We cannot forget that our Unitarian friends who hold only to *God as Father* are no worse off than some of my evangelical friends who speak of God only as *Son* or some of my Pentecostal friends who speak of God only as *Holy Spirit.* While in seminary, I was always slightly amused

[1] The last time I used this analogy I was accused of Sabellianism (the subtle heresy which implies three separate Gods) because I failed to emphasize Father, Son, and Holy Spirit as three manifestations of *one* God. Please, let this be understood.

[2] It should be said that these roles attributed to Father, Son, and Holy Spirit are primary, not exclusive. These roles are not only interrelated, they overlap. The Son, for example, has a great deal to do with the creation (John 1:3, Colossians 1:15, 18), a role primarily attributed to God the Father.

by those who spoke only of the fatherhood of God, the brotherhood of man, and the neighborhood of Boston. On the other hand, some of the most ardent critics of the lay witness mission movement are concerned because some few witnesses tend to isolate Jesus.[3] To isolate Jesus or to glorify only an experience with him gives him no glory at all. Remember, each role or function that God must perform must bear witness to the other. In John 16, when Jesus speaks of the Holy Spirit, he says, "He will glorify me, for he will take what is mine and declare it to you. All that the Father has is mine; therefore I said that he will take what is mine and declare it to you." As for my Pentecostal friends, frequently I walk into a Pentecostal church where there is no central display of the cross whatever; the Holy Spirit is the all-in-all. I'm not saying that you cannot worship God separately as Father, Son, or Holy Spirit. Certainly one person is not jealous of another. I am simply saying that the Holy Spirit must be understood as one with the Father and the Son.

In the final analysis, as Christians we believe in a triune God not simply because our Bibles tell us to but because our experiences of being led to the Father, through the Son, by the Holy Spirit also bear this out. Experiences must underscore scripture. So, when I speak of the Father, Son, or Holy Spirit in this book, you must remember that I am speaking of a total experience of Father, Son, and Holy Spirit. Furthermore, if I focus on

---

[3] In the lay witness mission movement, laymen travel at their own expense to witness in local churches outside their own communities.

the Holy Spirit it is only because he is a *present power* made available by the Father, through the Son.

Unfortunately, the Holy Spirit is easily misunderstood. He so easily becomes an "it" (which of course he is not), or some holy spook. His gifts are grossly abused. Yet, he is still the source of power in a world that desperately needs power to survive. So let's spell this out in terms of Christian experience. 10/6/74

PART II

The Holy Spirit in Christian Experience

Chapter III
Tingle When You Touch:
The Fruit of the
Holy Spirit Is Love

Recently a high school student came to my office asking exactly what it meant to be a Christian. As we talked, the conversation soon moved into the area of the Holy Spirit. When I began to explain the power available to Christians through faith in Jesus Christ she suddenly asked: "If everyone had this power, wouldn't the world be a madhouse of electricity? What would that be like?" I replied instantly: "That would be like heaven! We would all tingle when we touch."

I remember when I first fell in love; I hope you can too. I was about six. There was a cute little girl down the street, and when our hands touched, we tingled. The tragic thing is, we don't tingle much any more. We slip into our pews on Sunday morning and our elbows touch, but we rarely tingle. Far too many are separated people in a separated world. Relationships so hard to come by die so easily. It's difficult to keep love alive! Like the church at Ephesus to whom John the son of Zebedee is writing in Revelation 2, we have lost the tingle, we have lost our first love.

Yet, the fruit of the Holy Spirit is love, and love must not only be sustained, it must grow and grow and grow and grow. Few of us doubt that the only unimpeachable mark of the Spirit-filled life is love. Love is the stuff of which tingle is made, and "God's love has been poured into our hearts through the Holy Spirit which has been given to us" (Romans 5:5). Let's talk about love, first as the fruit of the Spirit which must then be sustained if we are to become, in the complete sense of the word, the partakers of the Holy Spirit.

Holy Spirit fruit is unmistakable. Matthew 7:17 talks about fruit. Matthew 12:33 is even more to the point: "Either make the tree good, and its fruit good; or make the tree bad, and its fruit bad; for the tree is known by its fruit." Spirit-filled Christians are known by their fruit. Galatians 5:22-23 says: "The fruit of the Spirit is love, joy, peace, patience, kindness, goodness, faithfulness, gentleness, self-control; against such there is no law." I have already said that *love* is the only real fruit of the Holy Spirit, so you might well ask, What about joy, peace, patience, etc.? My friend David Seamands said it: "These are simply adjectives for love, while love itself is the only unimpeachable fruit of the Holy Spirit."

If Galatians 5:22 identifies the fruit, then I John 4:7

spells it out: "Beloved, let us love one another; for love is of God, and he who loves is born of God and knows God." To know God is to be born of his Spirit, and to be born of his Spirit is to love. To put it another way, to know God is to "let God be God," and to let God be God is to tap the infinite reservoir of his love. To begin anywhere else is to miss the mark. Let me illustrate.

Our son, Eric, is almost two (I couldn't understand child abuse until we had a two-year-old). He knows when things aren't right between Pati and me. He can feel the tension. So how do I love him? I love Eric by first loving his mother, and out of that relationship I can properly love him. The same principle applies in our relationship with God. Some years back a young girl said to her fiancé: "Honey, of course you realize I love God more than I love you." My first reaction was shock (a bit of nausea, to be more honest), but then it dawned. This is not a competitive love; it's a complementary love. Only as she first loved God could she really love her fiancé. Out of our relationship with God, we love each other.

All right, what about this love, this fruit of the Holy Spirit? What is its nature? How does it manifest itself?

Without going into a long discourse on the different kinds of love implicit in the specific Greek words, simply let me say that we are not talking about sexual love—*eros*. Nor are we talking about the love for a friend—*philia,* nor love within the family—*storge*. As important as these kinds of love are, basically, they all find root within man. Here, however, we are talking about the kind of love described by the New Testament

37

word *agape,* and it is unique in that it finds its origin not within us, but in God.

The nature of *agape* is to expect nothing in return. Too many of us are frequently suspicious of this kind of love. We expect a "catch." Even in our relationship with God we want to get cleaned up before we let him love us. When I was a small boy I found myself saying, "Dad will love me *if* I am good." He didn't say that, but I got the message. Then when I grew up and realized that I was calling God "Father" I still found myself saying, "God will love me *if* I am good." The truth about *agape* is that our being good has nothing to do with God's loving us. We don't have to wait until we get cleaned up to let God love us. He loves us where we are. This "no strings" kind of love according to I John 4:18 is the "perfect love [which] casts out fear."

Fear can cripple us. Let me illustrate. Roberto Escamilla tells the story of watching some people dancing in the ballroom of the Chicago Hilton when suddenly he realized that they were all stone deaf. As I heard him tell that story I realized that I too must sometimes dance to music I cannot hear. I get depressed—maybe you do too—and no longer hear the music playing. My depression used to cripple me, but not anymore. Even though I still get depressed, because I now understand more fully the nature of God I've learned to dance to music I cannot hear.

I recently heard a well-known conference speaker refer to perfect love as perfect nonsense. We had better hope not! We know that God's love is perfect (surely it was this kind of love demonstrated on the Cross), and the New Testament exhorts us to keep this kind of love as a goal constantly set before us until our perfect love becomes like unto his perfect love. It is the Holy Spirit that moves us toward this goal—again, not a static, immovable goal, but a dynamic, ever improvable goal that keeps us churning inside, that keeps us excited about life and all its possibilities.

Again, perfect love is the only unimpeachable mark of the Spirit-filled life. Little wonder Christians for centuries have been debating its meaning. So let's see how others spoke about it, and then we can discuss its relevance for today with regard to becoming the partakers of the Holy Spirit.

If you had lived in the eighteenth century and were interested in the Spirit-filled life you would undoubtedly have been reading some rather obscure Roman Catholic mystics. Francois Fénelon (1651–1715), for example, was one of the first to articulate a theology of perfect love. Fénelon, the Archbishop of Cambrai, was his father's fourteenth child. As a small boy he had a deeply religious turn of mind. In 1678, he was appointed the head of a society for Catholic converts which also had the responsibility of instructing young women. Perfect love for Fénelon drew off all affections that were not first centered upon God, and granted perfect peace. It was a "disinterested" love. By disinterested we simply mean that it had no desire of its own. This is the very essence of the *agape* love we mentioned earlier. Motive enough for perfect love is that God first loved us. Perfect love

39

expects nothing in return. We love God and one another not that we may receive his good gifts nor even for the joy of loving, but simply because God is love and we would be restored in his image.

The primary reason, however, for mentioning Fénelon here is to explore his understanding of perfect love as process. Fénelon's well-known phrase *moi progressus ad infinitum* simply means that we grow *in* perfect love. To put it another way, what is perfect love today then must progress in order to be perfect love tomorrow. Perfect love is moving, never arriving, always looking for new ways of expressing itself, always looking for weaknesses to conquer, always looking for new ways of serving and always developing greater sensitivity to the needs of others.

Another such Roman Catholic mystic was Brother Lawrence (1605–1691). Born Nicholas Herman, he understood perfect love in terms of the continual practice of the presence of God. Brother Lawrence was not a gifted man in the sense that he had any great talent. Quite to the contrary, he never seemed to be able to do anything right. If anyone ever had two left feet and was all thumbs it was Brother Lawrence. At the age of forty-four he felt himself such a failure that he decided to punish himself by entering a Carmelite monastery in Paris, where he was immediately assigned to the kitchen as cook to the society. Although he was just as inept in the kitchen as he might have been elsewhere, those in charge felt that here he could do the least harm. Among the mundane chores of the kitchen Brother Lawrence decided to excel in one thing, the continual practice of the presence of God. Even while peeling mounds of potatoes he mastered this art and soon set an example for all in the society. At the time of his death his works were published, giving inspiration and hope to people the world over down through the centuries.

The point is this. Frequently I find myself doing things in the presence of God I would never do in the presence of others. Why? Simply because I am more keenly aware of God's creation than I am of God. Perfect love is being as keenly aware of God at all times as I am of his creation. I find it difficult to sin when I am most aware of God. It is therefore easiest to sin when I turn away from God. Someone made a poster for my office which reads: "If you are getting further from God, guess who is moving." Perfect love is acknowledging God in all things. As Christians we believe that all things relate to God or they relate to nothing. If I love you I acknowledge you, I listen and learn from you when we are together. I never take you for granted. I take our conversation seriously. Nothing irritates me more than to be talking to a person and find that after thirty seconds he is looking over my shoulder to see if there is someone else whose conversation would be more profitable. Perfect love means that God and all people are worth hearing and are to be treated with respect. Frank Laubach for two months practiced continually the presence of God. He remarked afterward that although keeping an awareness of God was the most difficult task of all, all other tasks came easily. Perfect love is never allowing the presence of God or others to be lost in the busyness of the day.

Gaston Jean Baptiste de Renty (1611–1649) was a wealthy French marquis. Motivated by perfect love, de Renty gave away all that he had and went to assist his fellow man in the bread lines of Paris, feeding the weak and impoverished. De Renty, like Brother Lawrence, lived with a constant awareness of God's presence. He defined perfect love in terms of complete dedication to God. This perfect love was vigorous and full of vitality. His life was a marvel of devotion to God and man. If ever we should doubt the effectiveness of genuine piety we should read de Renty. Surely purity of intention and affection, a wholehearted attitude to God, is the essence of perfect love.

Very briefly, let's review what all this has to do with becoming partakers of the Holy Spirit. First of all, sanctifying grace aims at perfect love. It's like God's love, which says even though you crucified my Son, I want you to have my Son's inheritance. Imagine walking into my home and murdering my two-year-old son in cold blood and my saying to you: "I not only forgive you for murdering my son, I want you to have my son's inheritance." You would think one of two things—either I was mad or I was for real. Somehow God is for real, and his love is perfect. Perfect love, however, is not some ultimate goal that we eventually attain and then stop growing. It is a process that is forever turning us to the life of the Spirit. I once served a church where one of my members nearly beat me to death (quite literally). I should hasten to add that I had some of it coming since I

42

made the mistake of getting out ahead of my people before I gave them a chance to love me. If you don't know that I love you, I walk softly in your life. The man who had beaten me drove a certain kind of automobile, and whenever I saw that kind of automobile (whether he was in it or not) something would tighten inside me. It was not until I was able, by the power of the Holy Spirit, to release the resentment that I was able to grow in the Spirit. Now when I see that certain make of automobile, so help me, I find love welling up.

Perfect love has no will of its own. Several months back I preached a youth revival where three hundred and fifty kids, ages fifteen to twenty-five, came to hear the gospel of Jesus Christ. One of the kids was simply unable to love. He held out until the last day, and when realizing that he had been loved, no strings attached, he was able to love. He ran around the camp telling everyone, "I can love, I can love."

Perfect love is sensitive to the presence and needs of others. It is response to reconciliation. I must confess that for several years it was extremely difficult for me to preach on love since most of what I was hearing on the subject seemed insipid; it seemed to have little or no integrity. God was love, love, love, and it didn't really matter what I did or did not do. Now there is some truth to this, since, as I have already said, God loves us where we are. Yet, in the final analysis, how can we talk about perfect love without dramatizing the necessity for a reasonable response to God in Jesus Christ having reconciled the world to himself?

I have for some time been fascinated by some mystics who interpret hell as the creation of God's love, not God's wrath. They imagine a man, "unwashed by the blood of Christ," standing before the blazing holiness of God presuming to plead his own case. He insists upon his innocence while standing there exposed, with his sins hanging out. Suddenly he is aware! He cannot bear the light, the awful exposure. He looks for cover, a tree to hide behind, a rock to crawl under, a mountain to fall upon him (Revelation 6:16). Some mystics say that God created the darkness of hell to give just such a man a place to hide. The comic strip entitled "Andy Capp" is about a despicable little English sot who is always getting into trouble. In a recent strip, Andy is chasing a woman, and as he passes the parish church he pops a penny in the "save our roof" fund box hanging on the door. The vicar comes out and somewhat untheologically says, "Thanks Andy, you'll go to heaven for that . . . but you won't like it." Andy wouldn't like heaven; he couldn't bear the light.

Finally, perfect love does not draw attention to itself. I remember someone once said of me that I was too pious. I immediately replied that rather I was not pious enough. Genuine piety is not for display, it doesn't draw attention to itself; it is for enabling us quietly and unassumingly to enjoy God forever. If I *were* truly pious, my piety would not have been so obvious.

Perfect love, therefore, never glorifies an experience, it is an experience that glorifies God in Jesus Christ. A couple of years ago I had the privilege of spending a week with E. Stanley Jones. For a half hour each day we would study a portion of scripture from the writings of Paul. The first day, Dr. Jones opened to the passage and said: "Paul dipped his pen in the blood of his broken heart and set pain to music." It was one of the most exciting weeks in my life. Shall I tell you what passage we studied? Read it carefully.

Love never ends; as for prophecies, they will pass away; as for tongues, they will cease; as for knowledge, it will pass away. For our knowledge is imperfect and our prophecy is imperfect; but when the perfect comes, the imperfect will pass away. When I was a child, I spoke like a child, I thought like a child, I reasoned like a child; when I became a man, I gave up childish ways. For now we see in a mirror dimly, but then face to face. Now I know in part; then I shall understand fully, even as I have been fully understood. So faith, hope, love abide, these three; but the greatest of these is love (I Corinthians 13:8-13).

10/6/74

Chapter IV
Desire the Higher Gifts: Wisdom, Knowledge, Discernment

Within the charismatic movement there are those who would emphasize the fruit of the Holy Spirit and those who would emphasize the gifts of the Holy Spirit. We have already said that the only unimpeachable mark of the Holy Spirit is love, and if you must emphasize one or the other then emphasize the fruit. Yet, the Holy Spirit will frequently manifest himself through various gifts as well. When one speaks of the gifts of the Holy Spirit, we frequently think of the nine gifts listed in the first eleven verses of I Corinthians 12. The gifts here, however, are not definitive. We must not—I repeat, we must not —limit the gifts of the Holy Spirit to those mentioned only in I Corinthians 12. These gifts, wonderful as they are, define only the range of the Spirit's gifts. There are many other gifts as well. Romans 12, for example, includes the gift of service or the gift of giving. The gift of teaching is listed not only in Romans 12 but again in Ephesians 4, which goes on to say that some are given special gifts as apostles, as evangelists, as pastors, but clearly all are given for building up of the body of Christ.

Although not all the gifts of the Holy Spirit are listed in I Corinthians 12, there has been much debate within the charismatic movement as to the range of these gifts. This and the next two chapters therefore will deal with these nine gifts one by one.

I believe that the gifts of the Holy Spirit are for today, that they are for the church, and that they are for you. They must, however, be grounded in love, never drawing attention to themselves, always glorifying God in Jesus Christ. Some of the Christians I admire most have been somewhat disillusioned by the abuse of the Spirit's gifts. E. Stanley Jones, for example, cautions against their divisiveness. Those who know Dr. Jones understand his caution. A great deal of his ministry was in India. There he was sick to death of Pentecostals making Pentecostals out of Christians rather than making Christians out of non-Christians. All too frequently, the gifts of the Holy Spirit lead to a kind of pride which interests itself more in proselyting than in evangelizing.

Others believe that the gifts of the Holy Spirit were for only another dispensation. Again, I believe that the gifts of the Holy Spirit are for today, partly because I find them in the New Testament and partly because I've seen with my own eyes. Unfortunately, most books deal only with a few of the gifts. Those which emphasize the more subtle gifts (wisdom and knowledge) frequently ignore

47

the more outwardly manifest ones (healing, working of miracles, speaking in tongues), and vice versa.

These chapters are designed to give equal emphasis to all the gifts in light of the Holy Spirit, "to apportion each one individually as he wills." After setting the historical context for I Corinthians 12-14, let's look at the gifts under this grouping. First: wisdom, knowledge, and discernment (the gifts of the Holy Spirit manifested through the *intellect*); second: faith, healing, and the working of miracles (the gifts of the Holy Spirit manifested through the *miraculous*); and finally: prophecy, tongues, interpreting tongues (the gifts of the Holy Spirit manifested through the *spoken word*).

Since we are dealing primarily with I Corinthians 12, I feel it is important to set the stage for the Corinthian Church. The founding of the church in Corinth is described in Acts 18:1-18. Paul went to Corinth from Athens. He stayed in the home of Priscilla and Aquila, who had recently come from Italy, and with them engaged in tentmaking. On the Sabbath he preached to both Jew and Gentile.

Corinth was relatively a new city. It was just one hundred years old. It was a city of the future. Consequently the Corinthians liked things that were new. They were impressed by things shiny and novel. They were impetuous, quick to explore new ideas, at least until the novelty wore off, and they then frequently fell away, lost interest, or corrupted the idea. They loved Apollos more than Paul, because Paul was earthy whereas Apollos was eloquent.

48

There were four letters in all written to the Corinthian Church. The first letter is missing. The second letter is our I Corinthians. The third letter, called the painful letter, can probably be found in II Corinthians, chapters 10 through 13. The fourth letter is then II Corinthians, chapters 1 through 9. I Corinthians, therefore, is actually Paul's second letter to the church at Corinth. Some of the Corinthians were abusing the gifts of the Holy Spirit, and here he is intending to give some direction in light of the teachings of Christ; but let's dig a bit deeper.

In the Old Testament (or old covenant) the Holy Spirit, by and large, acts *upon* us rather than *through* us as our lives had not yet been cleansed by the work of the Cross. Jesus, therefore, in John 13:31–16:33, just prior to the crucifixion, outlines the work of the Holy Spirit since the stage was being set for the Holy Spirit not only to act upon us but to indwell, to fill the vessel where sin was about to be rooted out (expiated). The effects of this indwelling power can be clearly seen in the lives of the disciples. After the crucifixion that scruffy bunch of bedouin disciples, who were always dickering as to who was to be first in the kingdom of God, who were forever sleeping when they should have been praying, deserted Jesus to the man. After the resurrection they returned to their trades. After Pentecost, however, something happened. They became bold. Under the anointing of the Holy Spirit they began preaching with authority. Significantly, it was at Pentecost that the gifts of the Holy Spirit first manifested themselves generally. It is with regard to these gifts that Paul writes I Corinthians, chap-

49

ters 12 through 14, seeking to give both direction and correction in light of their abuse.

The Corinthians were drawn to the more visible gifts. Anyone in love with novelty is prone to abuse, and Paul is calling for discipline. So Paul, beginning with the manifestations of the Spirit's gifts through the intellect, lists the entire range of gifts. (Do not press these three more general areas—the intellect, the miraculous, and the spoken word—into too neat a package.) The first mentioned is wisdom.

Wisdom

Paul implies that the first mentioned gifts are the higher gifts (I Corinthians 12:31), and if we *must* seek a particular gift then by all means start here. A good bit of I Corinthians deals with wisdom. The Corinthian Church is to seek true wisdom. Wisdom, like most Christian virtues, cannot be measured by worldly standards. "God chose what is foolish in the world to shame the wise, what is weak in the world to shame the strong, what is low and despised in the world, even things that are not, to bring to nothing things that are, so that no human being might boast in the presence of God" (I Corinthians 1: 27-29).

It is difficult to seize upon the kind of wisdom that seems to be foolishness to those around us. Several years ago I was completing some graduate work in Europe. My wife had returned to the States because of an illness, and I moved into the dormitory of an Anglican theological college in Bristol, England. Although I was not a student at the college, owing to the low enrollment, I and several others were allowed to live in. I moved next door to a young Oxford graduate who was teaching French in one of the private schools in Bristol. He was an atheist. I remember that during one of the very first conversations we had, he simply explained that I was not to discuss the demands of the New Testament. They were foolishness to him. He knew the Scriptures and had long since discarded them. I remember I was surprised at how easily I accepted this ground rule. Although I did not press him, I did manage to out-live him (and I am not speaking about longevity). I believe I can have more fun doing God's thing than you can doing your own thing. I out-loved him, I out-joyed him, I out-peaced him, I even out-funned him. After I was around this young man practically every day for three months, he suddenly asked if he could read my dissertation for punctuation since he had been an English major at Oxford. You can imagine how pleased I was since we are talking about nearly five hundred pages. To make a long story short, half way through my dissertation, a quotation from John Wesley, in a footnote, led him to Christ. I shall never forget the first letter I received from my friend Allan upon my return to the States. "You say that it takes courage and real intelligence to maintain a childlike faith; it is only now that I am beginning to realize how very true that is: The real difficulty lies not in attempts to define God, the indefinable, but in simply accepting him without qualification. It's difficult in a world which values sophistication and 'rationalism' to get out of the habit of subscribing to such values, but I am realizing more and more the folly of such values in face of my helplessness without God—it's a painful process, and I can't help trying to hang onto my old attitudes and beliefs instead of 'falling into God,' as Luther says.''

Let's review just for a moment. Wisdom here is not the wisdom of the world. Wisdom as a gift of the Holy Spirit has frequently been called foolishness by those around us. Allan learned a painful lesson. True wisdom is a childlike faith; it takes God at his word. Finally, wisdom most supremely is revealed in Jesus Christ (I Corinthians 1:24, 30). Now let's be more specific.

There is a wisdom of God and a wisdom of man. If God is omniscient then he knows all things. I have always loved the verse from Romans 11: "O the depth of the riches and wisdom and knowledge of God! How unsearchable are his judgments and how inscrutable his ways!" In man, however, wisdom, even as a supernatural gift, does not approach the wisdom of God. Rather, it involves a deeper insight (beyond the intellect of man), which puts fact or truth to best advantage. Notice, wisdom involves more than truth alone; it involves the dispensing of truth in such a way that truth is not only heard but accepted. Just because you know the truth (and even if the truth has set you free) there is no guarantee the world will listen. I remember when I took my first church, on the South Side of Chicago. I thought that this section of Chicago was still one of the nation's greatest problem areas because I had not yet arrived. I roared into the community like a lion. After two weeks I received a phone call one night from one of my parishioners saying that there was a man there who was going to shoot him if I didn't come and prevent it. I told him not to worry, that I was on my way and that I would have everything under control. When I arrived I promptly told the assailant that he was not going to shoot my church member, and he replied rather hastily: "Yes I am; what's more I am going to start with you." He stuck a cocked .45 under my nose, and all I wanted to do was throw up. I can to this day smell the oil from the barrel. I repeat, wisdom involves more than the knowledge of truth; it involves the dispensing of truth in such a way that truth can be heard and accepted.

Wisdom, or rather a lack of wisdom, has been a problem down through the ages. I recall one of John Wesley's letters to his brother Charles late in his ministry in which he wrote that he had just finished reading some of their earliest sermons preached at the beginning of the Evangelical Revival. Wesley comments: "A marvel they didn't stone us." When I returned from Europe I took a church in the rural South. That was a tremendous learning experience for me. I made some real mistakes. Many of the church stalwarts would say: "But preacher, we've been doing it this way for fifty years"; to which I would reply rather glibly, "I can't think of a better reason for changing it." That, my friends, is a classic example of a lack of wisdom. Contrast that with the wisdom of Nathan who caused David to pronounce his own condemnation concerning the affair with Bathsheba. Solomon was wise; who can forget the beautiful story of the two women and the baby? Much of the first few chapters of I Kings applauds Solomon's understanding of human nature. He also had an understanding of history and literature. Many of the popular proverbs are a work of genius. Again, wisdom quickens the insight in ways essential to discovering truth and dispensing justice.

Most of all, however, spiritual wisdom comes from God and must therefore be considered a gift of the Holy Spirit. Paul knew this all too well. He writes in the latter part of I Corinthians 2: "So also no one comprehends the thoughts of God except the Spirit of God. Now we have received not the spirit of the world, but the Spirit which is from God, that we might understand the gifts bestowed on us by God. And we impart this in words not taught by human wisdom but taught by the Spirit, interpreting spiritual truths to those who possess the Spirit."

Finally, wisdom, like all the spiritual gifts, must be grounded in love—in short, another adjective for love. James 3 sums it up: "The wisdom from above is first pure, then peaceable, gentle, open to reason, full of mercy and good fruits, without uncertainty or insincerity."

Knowledge

The second gift of the Holy Spirit mentioned in I Corinthians 12 is knowledge. Whereas wisdom deals with the insight that dispenses truth, knowledge deals with truth itself. Webster defines knowledge in terms of an "acquaintance with facts, truths, or principles as a result from study or investigation." It hardly needs to be said that where knowledge as a gift of the Holy Spirit is concerned, this does not tell the whole story.

Knowledge, like all of the gifts of the Holy Spirit, must also be grounded in love. Paul writes in I Corinthians 8: "Knowledge puffs up, but love builds up." Knowledge gained from purely independent study frequently leads to pride. Christians effect change in the hearts and lives of others because they have a relationship with the living God, not because they have some particular kind of knowledge. Knowledge as a gift of the Holy Spirit is just as high above the knowledge of the world as wisdom as a gift is above the wisdom of the world. Knowledge as a gift is confirmed by the word of God. Let me share with you a portion of a more recent letter from my young Oxford friend in England.

Allan is still teaching French in a private school in Bristol where he has begun study groups among his pupils. "Everything's bolted up for me since I was baptized in the Holy Spirit just after Easter. I feel a new awareness of the Lord's presence and power, and a real thirst to learn more; and greater courage and freedom in Christ. In school, we've just started having a weekly house meeting for Bible study and prayer in the evening, in addition to the Friday lunchtime meeting we already had. The house meetings have been wonderful, with prayer coming straight from the heart—no theological self-indulgence. Some of the kids are having a really tough time because their parents or friends are non-

Christians, because of divorce or emotional instability. They know that the Lord is the only answer, and their prayers reflect the depth of their need and the extent of their trust in him.'' I share this with you simply to make this point. The gift of knowledge soon leads to the study of the Scriptures. The gift of knowledge involves an almost insatiable appetite for the Word of God. I read like mad, frequently two or three books a week. The more I read, however, the more I am convinced that the only truth, absolute truth, is revealed in the Word of God. Oddly enough, I came to this conclusion after spending considerable time with one who calls himself an atheist.

I worked off and on for six months in the British Museum Reading Room in London. After being there for almost a week I noticed an American studying in one of the booths. The odd thing was, he never checked out a book. The British Museum Reading Room, like the Library of Congress or the Bibliotheque Nationale in Paris, supposedly contains every book published. For one to come every day to the Reading Room and never check out a book is rather odd indeed. I remember I would catch his eye. Occasionally we would smile but never speak, as I was busy and so was he. After a week of only smiling I decided I wanted to meet this interesting character since he was approximately my own age. I later found that he wanted to meet me as well, but neither one of us had the courage to speak up. Finally, one day in the coffee shop I took my cup of tea and scone to his table and after ten minutes or so of looking at each other and blushing, a conversation ensued. From that moment to this we've been the best of friends. My friend, I learned, was a full professor at one of our leading Western universities. The reason he never checked out a book, although he had already written three textbooks himself, was that he had become completely disillusioned with truth. According to him one book simply contradicted another. Even his own books contradicted themselves, and he was then writing a play on the meaning of life. After several weeks my friend convinced me too that there is no truth—at least, *apart from the Word of God!* As I hold the Word of God in my hand I say to myself: "Here is truth, and all other knowledge must be weighed in light of our understanding of these inspired pages." As Christians we weigh all things in light of our own understanding of the Scriptures. When I catch someone believing everything I tell him, I back off in a hurry. You weigh even the words on these pages in light of your own understanding of the Scriptures. Now, if you don't know the Scriptures, you are in trouble. You are afloat, and your task is clearly before you—to learn them, to hide them away in your heart. My friend in the British Museum was unable to accept the truth as revealed in the Word of God, but I did manage, so he said, to present him with the first reasonable alternative to his atheism. My, how I covet him for Jesus!

The Bible is the only book of balance. Here is knowledge, not just facts about the world we live in but truths about how one relates to the living God and those around him. The gift of knowledge, therefore, is the Holy Spirit enforcing the Word of God "supernaturally" in a number of different ways. Suddenly, in the midst of seeking a solution to a problem, insight comes. Kathryn Kuhlman, for example, claims the gift of knowledge more than the gift of healing. Suddenly she "knows" who has been healed among the body of believers.

The gift of knowledge dispels fear and overcomes doubt. We fear that which we do not understand, and we doubt that which we cannot approach intellectually. Most atheists suffer from a profound lack of knowledge as to the nature of things as they really are. I ask most atheists I meet to tell me about the god they don't believe in, and nine out of ten have thrown out some god I threw out ten years ago. The god they don't believe in I don't believe in either. Again, the gift of knowledge is the Holy Spirit enforcing the Word of God "supernaturally" so that we understand the nature of things as they really are. Little wonder Wesley required all his preachers to read the Scriptures and to pray at least five hours a day. He said, in effect: "If you don't want to read and pray five hours a day, learn to want to read and pray five hours a day. If you can't learn to want to read and pray five hours a day, gentlemen, return to your trades, for you'll be a trifler the rest of your days and a pretty superficial preacher."

Discernment

Although discernment is not the third gift listed in I Corinthians 12, it is so closely related to the Holy Spirit manifesting himself through the intellect, we will discuss it here.

For every good gift of God, Satan has a counterfeit. Mark 13:22 warns: "False Christs and false prophets will arise and show signs and wonders, to lead astray, if possible, the elect."

We must remember that in the first century the Scriptures were not easily available. There were few ways of checking a man's credentials against the Word of God. Someone needed to be able to discern, lest the church be led astray. Discernment, therefore, as a gift of the Holy Spirit, deals specifically with the ability to distinguish between that which is of God and that which is not of God.

Discernment has an interesting precedent in the Old Testament. The Old Testament is constantly exhorting the people to use discernment. We remember Solomon's prayer for an understanding mind that he might discern between good and evil. God replied: "Behold, I give you a wise and discerning mind" (I Kings 3:12). Daniel was said to have had discernment ten times better than the magicians, enchanters, and sorcerers. He interpreted Nebuchadnezzar's dream: "Not because of any wisdom that I have" (Dan. 2:30). The Old Testament precedent for discernment, therefore, relates discernment to knowledge. In the New Testament, however, discernment as a gift of the Holy Spirit also distinguishes between spirits. Peter, in Acts 5, discerned a lie in Ananias and Sapphira. Again, in Acts 8, Peter discerned the intent of Simon's heart. Paul, in Acts 13, filled with the Holy Spirit, looked upon the prophet Bar-Jesus and exposed him as a "son of the devil." There is a beautiful story in Acts 16 concerning a slave girl whose ability to tell fortunes was being exploited by her masters. They were becoming quite wealthy. When she encountered Paul, he sensed or discerned a wrong spirit and commanded the spirit to come out in the name of Jesus Christ, and upon her deliverance she was no longer able to tell fortunes. This angered her masters, and Paul was thrown into prison.

Since the Scriptures are today so easily available, some might think that the gift of discernment is not now nearly so prevalent as it was in the first century. There is no question in my mind that this is still an important gift. Satan has found perfect cover in our twentieth-century sophistication. Milton and Dante have done the church a great disservice by portraying the Grand Deceiver with horns and a tail. This image is so easily dismissed by the twentieth-century mind. No one who has read C. S. Lewis' *Screwtape Letters* can doubt the subtlety of Satan's approach. All too frequently he dresses as an angel of light. I am grateful for the gift that can expose such a charade. Even today we must test the spirits.

At this point, let me add a word of caution. Many in the charismatic movement have associated the gift of discernment with the ability to cast out demons. Let me say that I believe in demons. I have sensed the evil power that can attach itself to the mind, body, and spirit of the believer. We must—I repeat, *we must*—however, use extreme caution in dealing with such spirits! I need only to remind you of the story described in Acts 19 where the itinerant Jewish exorcists undertook to pronounce the name of the Lord Jesus over those who had evil spirits, saying, ''I adjure you by the Jesus whom Paul preaches.'' You remember the evil spirit answered, ''Jesus I know, and Paul I know; but who are you?'' The man who had the evil spirit then leaped upon the exorcists, overpowering them so that they were forced to flee out of the house naked and wounded. We must realize that to cast out an evil spirit means that he can then occupy something or someone else. The instruction of the *Didache* (which describes the teachings of the second-century church, A.D. 160) requires the demon to be bound and cast into the very depths of hell. Those who would cast demons out of everything that wiggles could well endanger the weaker parts of the body of Christ. Those who are able to cast out evil spirits must not only approach such a ministry with extreme caution but only after much prayer and fasting and by the power of the Holy Spirit.

Many of you are perhaps concerned with some kind of demonic possession. Demon possession is not so common as you might suppose. If you are reading this book I doubt very seriously that you are possessed by anything other than God's Holy Spirit.

Satan is on a tether. If, however, we slip within the reach or range of his tether, yielding to some particular temptation, he'll have us for breakfast. We are not helpless. Jesus Christ has given us the victory. Satan has no power of his own; yet, if we yield to him he can and will deceive us. Little wonder Deuteronomy 18 exhorts us so strongly against having anything at all to do with those who practice fortune-telling, or those who would communicate with the dead: "For whoever does these things is an abomination to the Lord; and because of these abominable practices the Lord your God is driving them out before you" (Deuteronomy 18:12). I beg you, treat anything that smacks of spiritualism with a discerning mind. If you have a fortune-telling board, get rid of it! Satan exploits the voided mind.

Spiritualism or an interest in the spirit world can all too easily diminish our relish for the Scriptures. Too many of my friends who are busily communicating with the spirits of another dimension have soon gotten above the Scriptures and now interpret the Word of God in light of some "spirit communication." I am firmly convinced that this kind of misguided interest can easily lead into the occult.

I have a similar uneasiness about astrology. Astrology is an attempt to use the stellar bodies of the universe to foretell the future. It is at least as old as the ancient Babylonians (3200 B.C.) and is not to be dismissed lightly as mere superstition. The scriptures clearly warn against its abuses, however: "You are wearied with your many counsels; let them stand forth and save you, those who divide the heavens, who gaze at the stars, who at the new moons predict what shall befall you. Behold, they are like stubble, the fire consumes them; they cannot deliver themselves from the power of the flame" (Isaiah 47:13-14). Again, Jeremiah 10:2-3 reads: "Don't act like the people who make horoscopes and try to read their fate and future in the stars! Don't be frightened by predictions such as theirs, for it is all a pack of lies. Their ways are futile and foolish'' (TLB). If there is anything good to be gained from astrology and the like, only discernment can make the difference.

I have already stated that the nine gifts listed in I Corinthians 12 are not definitive. These gifts depict only the range of the Spirit's gifts. Wisdom, knowledge, and discernment, for example, are manifested through the intellect. It is important to remember that the Holy Spirit does not bypass the intellect; rather, the intellect yields to the will of God. There are other gifts, however, now to be considered which manifest themselves still differently. *10/7/74*

Chapter V
God Would Have Us Dreaming: Faith, Healing, Working of Miracles

We now move to the more visible gifts of the Holy Spirit. If wisdom, knowledge, and discernment are manifested through the intellect, then faith, healing, and the working of miracles are manifested through the miraculous.

Faith

When I was a sophomore in college it suddenly dawned on me that if there was no God, all my praying would one day mark me a fool. Since no college sophomore wants to be marked a fool I stopped praying, at least as a regular habit. For nearly two years the lines of communication between God and me were seldom used. Frequently, haunting doubt depressed me. I felt vulnerable. In a previous chapter I described my conversion, which was to take place nearly two years later, but the vulnerability didn't end there either. In a very real sense, even after conversion, we are still being saved. We have already established that the experience of rebirth is only the beginning of a lifelong Christian adventure. Several months after the new life in Christ had begun I was still plagued by fits of doubt. Suddenly, and apparently for no reason, just for a moment, I would wonder if there was a God and if the experience I had had with Christ was real. At one point my prayer life became difficult and my devotions seemed dull and routine. Finally, one night in desperation I stayed awake to pray. I have sometimes jokingly remarked that I have not prayed all night since because I am afraid that the Holy Spirit really would get me. At any rate, just about dawn, for the first time in my life, I felt the peace that passes understanding. I was almost overwhelmed by a greathearted and unquestioning trust in God. I felt the war within me had been won. That was over ten years ago, and from that moment till this I have not for a split second had a moment's doubt about God's presence in my life and God's presence in the world. This is a part of the gift of faith. I didn't deserve it. I certainly didn't earn it. I rarely speak about it. Yet it's there. God somehow sensed a need in me. It was then that I began to realize that the gifts of the Holy Spirit are not just for the spiritual, but for the needy as well.

Let me hasten to add that the gift of faith involves not only an awareness of God's presence, but a kind of trust in God which steps out believing. Somehow God is in control! We belong not to ourselves, we belong to him;

and since we belong to him he will provide all things necessary for the abundant life. The Bible talks about God as the source of all things. God is the source of my income, for example. The great church that I serve is only the instrument. Although I am grateful for the instrument it can never be more than the instrument. The moment I believe that this church is the source of my income, I begin to tell these good people what they want to hear, not what they need to hear, and I'm no longer any good to them. God will provide. The Scriptures say it. Faith confirms it in our hearts. If this instrument of income is taken away, then surely God will raise up another. I am at God's mercy, no one else's; and because I believe that he loves me, I can with confidence press on toward the mark of being his Spirit-filled person.

All Christians have *saving* faith because all Christians have the Holy Spirit, which enables us to believe. The gift of faith, however, is more constant; it believes that God's grace is sufficient. The *gift* of faith is at its best when things are worst. I remember when I was a boy my father used to say that "some folks feel worst when they feel best because they know how bad they're going to feel when they feel worst again, whereas some folks feel best when they feel worst because they know how good they're going to feel when they feel best again." The gift of faith has a great deal to do with perspective.

Faith knows the mind of Christ. It somehow knows that God is Father. It never loses heart. I sometimes lose patience with those who would cite the portion of the Passion narrative where Christ cries out, "My God, my

God, why hast thou forsaken me?'' as apparent proof that he too lost hope. I do not believe it! Surely, he was fully a man, but faith even among men never loses hope. Remember that the Orthodox Jew frequently quotes the Psalms from beginning to end during times of crisis. A great deal of light can be shed upon the Passion narrative when we realize that Jesus, during the entire sequence of events that led to his crucifixion, was reciting the Psalms. "My God, my God, why hast thou forsaken me?" is a direct quote from Psalm 22:1. Are we really surprised that the Gospel writer thought this appropriate enough to be quoted? The end is not despair however. Read on through the Psalms stopping at Psalm 31:5 where we find the words: "Into thy hand I commit my spirit." There is the gift of faith, there is the mind of Christ.

Faith knows how to dream and to dream big. I serve a church with over six thousand members. I'm grateful that the New Testament doesn't condemn bigness. Faith knows the Word of God and stands upon its promises with confidence and trust. I have already said that the spiritual gifts discussed in this chapter manifest themselves through the miraculous. In the final analysis, the gift of faith is the supernatural enhancer. "By faith Enoch was taken up so that he should not see death" (Hebrews 11:5). "By faith Sarah herself received power to conceive, even when she was past the age" (Hebrews 11:11). "By faith the people crossed the Red Sea as if on dry land; but the Egyptians, when they attempted to do the same, were drowned. By faith the walls of Jericho

fell down after they had been encircled for seven days"
(Hebrews 11:29-30). By faith some have built great
churches. By faith some have begun great universities.
By faith some have dared to accept challenges far beyond
their means. I think of a great church in the West, begun
just a few years ago by a man with a vision and only a
handful of people, which now has an influence throughout one of our greatest metropolitan areas. I am thinking
of a university in the Southwest built on a dream, a
kingdom dream, meeting tremendous need. I am thinking of a man who dared to accept the call of a ministry to
the drug culture in the East which has spread across our
land. Surely this is the gift of faith.

Faith somehow rises above the situations that are just
too big for ordinary prayer. The gift of faith is something
of a vision in itself. I'm reminded of Jesus in the garden,
the gift of faith that looked beyond the Cross to the "joy
set before him."

Healing

Spiritual healing was thought commonplace in the first
century. If you were sick and you were a Jew, you went
to the Rabbi, no questions asked. The climate was right.
Today, however, things are different. Not many would
believe that God heals physically even if they were to see
it. For modern man an immanent God who is intimately
concerned with the welfare of his children, spiritually,
emotionally, and physically, has been replaced by scien-
tific skills. Even our nursery rhymes have been rewritten:

God Would Have Us Dreaming

Twinkle, twinkle, little star,
I know precisely what you are.
I know your size, I know your mass,
You're not a diamond, you're helium gas.

Somehow our miserable little world has shrunk to the place where it can acknowledge only those things which can be logically deduced. This is not to disparage science. Many of the world's greatest scientists have a profound faith in God. It's the lesser mind that dares not build upon a mystery. It's the lesser mind that fails to recognize man as a whole.

I frequently hear Christians talking about saving souls. I agree, but I hasten to add that we Christians must come to grips with just what there is about a man that is worth saving. Is it just his "soul" (like some nebulous substance that, if placed under an ultraviolet light, could be removed like an appendix), or is it body and mind as well? The Hebrew concept of body and soul is one of totality. It begins with the story of creation. God in Genesis 2 is seen as the potter who molds man from clay, and breathes into the molded image the breath of life, and man becomes a "living soul." Notice, God does not put a soul into the clay. The clay becomes a living soul. Soul, translated from the Hebrew word "nephesh" means person—*body, mind,* and *spirit.* Throughout the Old Testament *nephesh* enter and die in battle. Need I remind you that men, not spirits, die in battle? Such as he is, man, in his total essence, is a soul—body, mind, and spirit. So if we are to minister to souls we are to minister

69

to persons, not just spiritually but physically and emotionally as well. Montaigne urged his contemporaries to train their limbs no less than their brain. It's not the body or the mind that we educate, but man. Little wonder Matthew 8:17 reads, "He took our infirmities and bore our diseases," as if to say that physical and emotional healing are as much a part of the atonement as spiritual healing.

Yet the church has neglected the healing sacrament. Unction, although still a healing sacrament in the Eastern Church (at least nominally), is now only a sacramental preparation for death in the Roman Catholic Church. I long for the day when the church will expect physical and emotional healing just as readily as it would conversion or the new birth. God obviously uses medical doctors. He wants to share the joy of healing. It would be an incredibly dull world if God did it all himself. So where science leaves off, the Holy Spirit can and will step in even more significantly.

I remember when in Chicago before I had even heard of the charismatic movement I preached a sermon on Thanksgiving eve. One of my members had been carried into the church with crippling arthritis. At the close of the service he threw away his crutches and ran to the altar. It nearly scared me to death, but he had been healed. I've never professed the gift of healing, but there's no question in my mind that I've seen it with my own eyes. My wife grew up on a blanket in an Oral Roberts tent. Frequently in the Midwest, where fish are not readily accessible, large goiters form as a result of the lack of iodine. My wife has described goiters disappearing before her eyes.

What of the church's philosophy of healing? What have we a right to expect? A mother comes to me and says that she has not faith enough to take her diabetic child off insulin. I respond in horror that only the doctor takes the child off insulin. God *heals,* and the physician *confirms.*

There are over twenty-six accounts of healing in the New Testament, not counting the parallel passages. There were undoubtedly many, many more. John reminds us that "there are also many other things which Jesus did; were every one of them to be written, I suppose that the world itself could not contain the books that would be written" (John 21:25). From these accounts I have arrived at the following philosophy of healing.

God heals for two reasons: to create faith, and that we might be more effective instruments in the kingdom of God. Healing is not only the result of faith; it must create faith, lest we be found guilty of ungratefulness like the nine lepers in Luke 17 who refuse to return and give praise to God. Second, God heals that we might be more effective instruments in his kingdom. For some, although God would have us whole our infirmity is a necessary reminder that God's grace is sufficient. Paul writes in II Corinthians 12 that God's "power is made perfect in weakness." Christians, as long as they remain in the world, have got to be willing to minister from weakness as well as from strength.

The gift of healing involves faith. To *initiate* healing,

however, faith is necessary only on the part of the one being used as the instrument for healing, not on the part of the one being healed. Just over one-half of those healed in the New Testament had faith in Christ. Many of them had never heard of Jesus; many were not even seeking healing, at least not from him. I repeat, faith is necessary only on the part of the one who is being used as the instrument for healing to *initiate* healing. Remember the story in Matthew 17 where Jesus says to the disciples that they were unable to cast out the demons because they had little faith? No one can say to you that you have not been healed because you had not enough faith.

At this point, however, let me hasten to add that faith is necessary on the part of the one who is being healed to *sustain* healing. Let me illustrate. Not too long ago I was standing in a trout stream fishing late in the day. Just as I was ready to leave the stream I caught a good size German brown. Since it was so late in the day I gutted him on the spot and placed him in my creel. He was dead. There can be no question about that, but he wiggled for fifteen minutes. As I walked back to the car I suddenly realized that dead diseases, like dead fish, can continue to wiggle. I used to pray for healing and the next morning when I felt the wiggle, I lost faith, assuming that God had not healed me. Now when I claim healing, in the name of Jesus and through the power of his Spirit, the next morning if I still feel the pain I simply pray for faith to outlast the wiggle. You would be amazed at the difference this has made. I have increasingly come to believe that persistence (faith outlasting the wiggle) is a necessary ingredient for spiritual healing. Jacob wrestled with God all night, saying: "I will not let you go, unless you bless me" (Genesis 32:26). I am reminded of the woman and the unrighteous judge, and how she persisted until justice was hers: "And will not God vindicate his elect, who cry to him day and night? Will he delay long over them?" (Luke 18:7.) My, how God loves a hungry heart!

The gift of healing is given by God to those who are open to this kind of ministry and who have need of this gift to minister in a particular situation. There are some puzzling questions concerning this gift, however. God's timing is one. Certainly God sometimes tarries to purify our motive. Too many want healing for the wrong reason—not to be a more effective instrument in the kingdom of God, but that they might become comfortable. Second, God sometimes tarries to intensify desire. We must want to be healed badly enough to accept the added responsibility that healing brings. If you accept the gift you belong to the Giver. Finally, God tarries to increase our ultimate joy. Some of our greatest blessings are a long time coming!

A more difficult question to answer is why God *apparently* heals some and not others. I am convinced that many of us are being healed every day and just don't realize it. Many of you who read these words have been healed hundreds of times. To say that God does not always heal, I think, misses the point. We have a healing service in our church every Saturday morning. There was a woman who came to this service week after week. One evening she died. As I preached her funeral service, suddenly it dawned on me that she had been healed a hundred times; she should have been dead ten years ago. All of us are being healed of some present infirmity whether we realize it or not; but, ultimately, healing is living in the presence of God, in a timelessness, having fellowship with the One who first loved us.

To conclude this section, let me share with you a brief description of our healing service. On Saturday mornings, at ten o'clock, we have a group that has been meeting for over two years. The service primarily glorifies God. Too many of the healing services that I have attended have digressed into "gripe sessions" for our latest ailments. Our group, however, begins by praising God. We read a psalm or some other act of praise. We then have a period of silent prayer when we prepare ourselves for God's healing Spirit. We pray in four parts. This is not so much a ritual as a design, that during the period of silence we might keep our minds on the task at hand. The first part concerns meditation where we concentrate on some healing event as revealed in the Scriptures. We meditate to the place where we can see Jesus in a particular situation healing the infirm. After we are able to see him clearly in our minds then we acknowledge his immediate presence among us. At this time we have a period of contemplation where, without words, we simply worship him. The twenty-third psalm affirms God without asking for a thing. After a time of worshiping God's Son we then speak to him out of our own personal need. I allow those in the service at this point to pray only for themselves. Finally, we listen; we listen to what God has to say to us on that particular morning. We try to give each part equal time.

A time of testimony follows the silent prayer. Each testimony must be relevant and up-to-date. We share what God is doing in our lives with regard to his healing ministry.

The psalm, the silent prayer and the testimonies take approximately three-quarters of an hour. Then and only then do we make intercession. We field requests from individuals in the group, and someone volunteers to pray specifically for each request. After each request has been fielded and accepted by someone in the service, we then have our circle of prayer. While in the circle of prayer, some there might request the laying on of hands, at which time several will gather, again invoking God's healing Spirit. Then at the conclusion of the service I frequently anoint each one, using oil and making the sign of the Cross on the forehead, simply praying: "In the name of the Father, the Son, and the Holy Spirit, be healed." We then conclude the service by singing some relevant benediction. Let me simply say that, after two years, this service is enormously meaningful to me! I've seen miracles.

Working of Miracles

Much of the groundwork for this section has already been laid. It is necessary, however, to mention a few things that apply specifically to this spiritual gift.

75

As I read the Scriptures I find two kinds of miracles. One kind supersedes natural law. The loaves and the fishes or the raising of the dead are classic examples. A second kind of miracle concerns timing. Although by natural means, the sea opened for the children of Israel at just the right moment to save a nation. The jail doors swung open, again by natural means, but at just the right moment to deliver the apostles.

Faith again is related to the working of miracles. Remember in Matthew 14 when Peter dared to step out onto the water, only to take his eyes off the Christ when he saw the wind blowing? The response of Jesus must have stung Peter: "O man of little faith, why did you doubt?"

Like healing, miracles are used of God both to create faith and to make us more effective instruments in his kingdom. No gift draws attention only to itself. The gift of working of miracles, like all the gifts, gives glory only unto God. Again, in John 20:30-31: "Now Jesus did many other signs in the presence of the disciples, which are not written in this book; but these are written that you may believe that Jesus is the Christ, the Son of God, and that believing you may have life in his name."

10/8/74

Chapter VI
The Holy Spirit and the Spoken Word: Prophecy, Tongues, Interpreting Tongues

The last three gifts we will discuss from I Corinthians 12 are manifested through the spoken word. A friend of mine recently pointed out that God in Genesis 1 simply said the Word and his creation sprang into life. James 3:6 reads: "And the tongue is a fire." With it we can bless the Creator or curse his creation. I am not surprised that God should include the range of the spoken word among the gifts of the Spirit.

Prophecy

Prophecy finds its beginnings in Deuteronomy 5. Here we find the story of a people who feared God. They dared not speak his name. In fact, the Hebrew word for "God" literally translates "The"—a strange name for Lord of the universe. These same people could not even bear to hear the sound of his voice. They asked God for a mediator, one who would speak his word that they might receive his word without fearing his presence. So, quite simply, they said: "God, take Moses to the mountain and give your message to him that he might return and give it to us." The prophet, therefore, is a herald, or a messenger of the divine Lord. He is one who sets forth the will of God to the people. He is one who cries: "Thus says the Lord" (or its modern equivalent). His message in turn is not just predictive or foretelling, but preaching, proclaiming! The gift of prophecy, therefore, is to receive from God insight into his purposes so that one speaks with authority regarding the present or future state of affairs.

One, for example, who can predict *with force* the consequences of religious decline has the gift of prophecy. He or she can see long before others a turn of events. Frequently the prophet is both misunderstood and mistreated. No one liked Noah. The prophet sees life the way some of us have seen movies, coming in at the very end. As we watch the earlier parts we sometimes feel the urge to leap onto the screen and shout, "Don't do it, it's a lousy ending." The prophet under the influence of the Spirit sees consequences and pleads with his people to turn away from some present course. He has a feeling for hidden trends and can weigh their results.

Again, the prophet speaks the Word of God. Prophecy is not interpretation; it must be the actual Word of God, without modification. "But the prophet who presumes to speak a word in my name which I have not commanded him to speak, or who speaks in the name of other gods, that same prophet shall die'' (Deuteronomy 18:20). This is not to say that the prophet cannot interpret. It is simply to say that the prophecy itself must be the "naked" truth. That which follows "thus says the Lord" must be directly from God.

The examples of prophecy in the Old Testament are numerous. Elijah received from God insight concerning his triumph over pretentious false worship. Amos portrays a God, righteousness alive, who will expose false security but will grant restoration and prosperity for the penitent. The prophecy of Hosea depicts a God pursuing a nation thoroughly depraved but whose divine love promises restoration to the penitent. Micah speaks the Word of God which requires humble and gracious service to human need and opens fellowship to those who will turn from ways of pride. Isaiah not only predicts the coming of a messiah, but announces faithfulness as the way to holiness: "Thou dost keep him in perfect peace, whose mind is stayed on thee, because he trusts in thee" (Isaiah 26:3). Ezekiel, under the words "the hand of the Lord is upon me," predicted the restoration of the temple and the river of life running from it.

Prophecy, like the other gifts of the Spirit, has been given to create faith and to equip the saints. It comes in the form of both warning and promise. Prophecy, first of all, awakens the godless but promises deliverance to those who will obey the will of God. Elijah warns Ahab against an alliance with Jezebel. Isaiah warns Israel against a similar alliance with Egypt when threatened by an Assyrian invasion. Both, however, promise deliverance if they will but turn to God. Warning and promise, warning and promise, such was the nature of prophecy. In fact, prophecy is the guardian of faith until we see face to face and faith is no more. In other words, prophecy confirms much of what we already believe and gives direction to the application of faith in our everyday lives.

The gift of prophecy has been granted by God to the entire body of Christ. Frequently, where there is sufficient freedom to prophesy in the setting of worship, there will be two or three prophecies. One prophecy will build upon the other. They will accrue, one stating a fact, another confirming that fact, and still another bringing it home.

It should be said that Jesus Christ is the fulfillment of *all* prophecy. The Old Testament is now interpreted through him. Abraham, you remember, was saved by faith in the promise to come, whereas you and I are saved by faith in the promise fulfilled. Jesus Christ is the real event! All prophecy must focus upon him. A prophet, therefore, must manifest more and more the mind that was in him.

This last point prompts a few thoughts regarding the character of the prophet. The prophet has been called the holy man. Remember, holiness either changes or consumes us. One never dabbles with the holiness of God. So the prophet is the one in the community who is so imbued with the love and righteousness of God as to sense with complete urgency the people's duty to respond. I love a description in Deuteronomy 34:10: "And there has not risen a prophet since in Israel like Moses, whom the Lord knew face to face." This description of Moses, whom God knew face to face, suggests that the prophet is one who lives in such close communion with God that he knows his mind, heart, will, and intent to the point that he can communicate them to men. The power to prophesy, therefore, depends directly upon the faithfulness of the prophet to whom the absolute holiness of God is all in all.

Tongues

This section is one of the ones I wanted to write most, because this is one of the gifts that has been manifested in my own experience the longest. I refuse, however, to speak about tongues without placing it within the context of the whole range of the Spirit's gifts and more especially the Corinthian correspondence. Since we have done our homework it is now time to discuss speaking in tongues.

First, let me say that speaking in tongues is not only a part of my experience, I also believe this gift to be a legitimate manifestation of the filling of the Holy Spirit. Pentecost first relates the experience. Acts 2:4: "And they were all filled with the Holy Spirit and began to speak in other tongues, as the Spirit gave them utterance." This same passage goes on to say that as a result of these *other* tongues, each person there heard the gospel proclaimed in his own language. These tongues could clearly be identified as known languages. Later on, however, and throughout the book of Acts, we find certain manifestations of tongues where there is apparently no one to identify the language—thus the expression *unknown tongues.*

In my own experience I frequently describe tongues like this. There are times in my devotional life when I can no longer find words to express my "innards." I am sure that you may have felt the same way at times. At that point I allow the Holy Spirit to pray through me in a language that I did not learn. Believe me, I know what it means to learn a language. I struggle with the biblical languages every day. I've heard David Seamands say on occasion that he knows a little Greek and a little Hebrew—one owns a restaurant, and the other owns a delicatessen. At any rate, I allow the Holy Spirit to pray through me in a language that I did not learn. I say a language because I believe it to be a language. My vocabulary is growing. I know enough about languages to be able to identify sentence structure. My unknown tongue or prayer language has periods, commas, and exclamation points. It is a marvelous gift, sometimes exhilarating, as I suddenly have an awareness of God's presence in my life: "Likewise the Spirit helps us in our weakness; for we do not know how to pray as we ought, but the Spirit himself intercedes for us with sighs too deep for words" (Romans 8:26). Tongues, however, are *not to be abused.* Let me explain.

Most of I Corinthians 14 was written by Paul to give both direction and correction to the gift of tongues. Here Paul discusses two apparent uses for tongues. One, for private devotions: "For one who speaks in a tongue speaks not to men but to God"; and "he who speaks in a tongue edifies himself." Second, the gift of tongues can be used in an open assembly, provided no more than three speak consecutively and there is always an interpretation for each manifestation.

I remember the first time I spoke in tongues. It was in an Episcopal church in Wheaton, Illinois. In a little chapel just the pastor and I knelt to pray. As he laid hands on me the tongue came; it's as simple as that. No one massaged my throat. No one tried to put words in my mouth. No one was telling me that I had to speak in tongues to be filled with the Holy Spirit. There was no real show of emotion. Just a few words came. I spoke them in faith and then was asked to interpret. Not realizing that one could interpret his own tongue I was somewhat surprised. But even as I was thinking upon the words that I had spoken I began to realize what I had said. The interpretation for my first words in tongues was this: "My poor, poor little boy; my, how you struggle." God wasn't laughing, but he was amused. Somehow, God and I have been closer ever since. Again, I didn't deserve the gift. I certainly didn't earn it. I rarely speak about it. Yet, it is there that I might have added strength for becoming a partaker of the Holy Spirit. So, why so much talk about *divisiveness?*

Divisiveness is a result of pride. There are two kinds of people who speak in tongues. For some, the gift has somehow made them haughty. They say to themselves, "I finally got spiritual enough for God to give me tongues." Rubbish! God gives gifts to the needy (as you would give money to the poor). For others, however, the gift has made them humble. While studying in Europe I preached every other Sunday in Methodist churches, but on the Sundays that I was not preaching I was at the feet of a little Pentecostal Scotsman who filled my cup. He had no education to speak of, but he had humility and when he spoke I listened. Why is there, then, such divisive pride?

Unfortunately, classic Pentecostal theology teaches that you must speak in tongues to be filled with the Holy Spirit. So help me, I've searched the Scriptures from cover to cover and nowhere can I find any passage where tongues are even alluded to as the unmistakable mark of the Spirit-filled life. Furthermore, I will not have God's children feeling like second-class Christians because they do not speak in tongues. If this were true, would not God have spelled it out? When the book of Acts refers to being filled with the Holy Spirit, sometimes tongues are mentioned, sometimes they are not. Check it out! I have the gift of tongues, but if you think for a moment that I have more Holy Spirit than some of my friends who I know to be far deeper into God than I am or perhaps ever will be, then you are dreaming. I know better. I have friends who have never spoken in tongues who have forgotten more about the Holy Spirit than I will ever know. Men of God have been moved by the power of his Spirit without the gift of tongues.

Let me share with you my first introduction to tongues. In an earlier chapter I described how I met my wife. What I did not say is that she is Pentecostal. She is a Methodist Pentecostal, and I am a Pentecostal Methodist. After we had dated for nearly a year, she began to describe her experience in the Holy Spirit. When I visited her church and several individuals spoke in tongues she began to relate to me this part of her own experience. At that time I had hardly even heard of the Holy Spirit. You can imagine my curiosity. This is the way she explained it. She described to me, much as I have just described to you, the Spirit of God praying through the Christian in an unknown tongue. She said, "Honey, I don't know why God gave me the gift of tongues, at least not exactly. What I do know is this. This gift helped me through some pretty rough adolescent years and it just seems that God, recognizing my weakness, gave me the gift of tongues in order to keep me where you are." As you can imagine, I was completely disarmed. Where's the pride in that? This I believe: *If you are as open to the Holy Spirit as I am, and if I have tongues and you don't, then I was weaker than you and God has given me something to keep me where you are.* The gifts are perhaps God's way of taking up slack. Many of us seem to fight more difficult battles. God knows what gifts we have need of and as we are open to his Holy Spirit, he will give us the gifts necessary to become partakers of the Holy Spirit.

Do not confuse any gift with the end. Even to be Spirit-filled is not to have arrived. We must keep moving. If you think that having tongues or any of the gifts is to have reached perfection once and for all then I pray to

God that you never receive them. We must not confuse the road with the destination.

The gifts are gifts, just that, nothing more. They are not wages. We do not earn them. God senses our need, in fact our weakness, and grants us the gifts sufficient to fulfill the ministry we have accepted where we are. Tongues cannot be exalted, but having said that, I should also add they cannot be forbidden either. Rather, we would yield to God's "Spirit, who apportions to each one individually as he wills" (I Corinthians 12:11).

Interpreting Tongues

I Corinthians 14:13 reads: "Therefore, he who speaks in a tongue should pray for the power to interpret." Since we have already touched on the necessity for interpretation in our discussion of tongues let me just reiterate a few of the points made there. Whenever tongues are used in an open assembly there must be an interpretation. If you have ever heard tongues spoken without an interpretation, someone was out of order. I remember I was speaking in a church where at the conclusion of the service someone rose and spoke in tongues. There was a sweetness about the tongues, and I felt the person was in order. At the conclusion of the message, however, no one interpreted. I remember praying: "Lord, someone's out of order; this man's message must be interpreted." Then, like a flash, I knew who was out of order. *I* was out of order, and immediately the interpretation came and I shared it with the congregation.

There must also never be more than three speakers for one assembly, and each must have a separate interpretation.

Finally, the interpretation usually comes in the form of prophecy, since the Holy Spirit is the one praying and the interpretation comes from him, not the individual. Furthermore, it is *interpretation,* not *translation.* Don't bother counting words. The interpretation might be twice as long as the message in tongues. It doesn't matter. Interpretation takes the message and not only puts it into English but drives it home by the power of the Holy Spirit.   10/9/74

Part III

The Holy Spirit in the World

Chapter VII
Pressed Down, Shaken Together, Running Over: The Holy Spirit in the Service of Reconciliation in the Church

Recently I was met at the airport by a man who drove me to a conference on the Holy Spirit. While we were riding, he asked, "Bob, how can I get more of the Holy Spirit? I've just got to get more." I responded, "What are you doing with what you've already got?" His silence was condemning. I simply cannot understand the kind of spirituality that would want more Holy Spirit while it has not yet put to work what it already has. Too many of us are seeking more while we're not yet using what we have. God doesn't equip freight trains to pull little red wagons. Our task, therefore, is clear. We must put what we have to good use, and then as we have need of more to be an even greater instrument in the kingdom, God will grant it. Luke 6:38 is the key: "Give, and it will be given to you; good measure, pressed down, shaken together, running over, will be put into your lap." Let me illustrate.

Very frequently I am asked: "Should I seek the gifts of the Holy Spirit?" My answer is: "No, at least not without *first* seeking the Giver." Everyone has the right to ask (especially for the higher gifts), but only God has the right to give and he "apportions to each one individually as he wills" (I Corinthians 12:11). Please, do not anticipate the mind of God. He alone knows the gifts that we need most. You ask then: "Is there nothing we can do to receive the gifts of the Holy Spirit?" Quite to the contrary, there is quite a bit we can do. We can *put to work* what we already have, and, as we have need of more, *believe* that God will grant whatever gifts are necessary to fulfill that particular ministry. Now, we need to offer some practical suggestions. We must constantly be looking for ways of serving, giving, or putting to work what we already have. There is a penetrating story in Mark 7.

Jesus has just been hassling with the Jewish elders. Finally, weary of the debate, he withdraws into the region of Tyre and Sidon where he enters the home of a friend to eat and to rest. Just as the table is being prepared, a woman enters whose daughter has been possessed by an unclean spirit. She pleads with Jesus to cast the demon out of her daughter. Then Jesus says a strange thing: "Woman, surely you don't expect me to take bread which belongs to the children and cast it to the dogs?" May I tell you what I would have said if Jesus had called me a dog? I would have said, "Jesus, take that religion of yours and shove it." Now listen to what the woman said: "Master, even the dogs eat crumbs that fall from the children's table." I think that's beautiful. Imagine such incredible faith. So what's the point? Like a flash one morning the thought occurred: *If crumbs can cast out demons, yea even raise the dead, what are we doing with the whole of the loaf?* When I see Christians, I see marvelous potential. I see freight trains. Yet, too many freight trains are pulling little red wagons. Let's spell this out. What is the Holy Spirit in the service of reconciliation really all about?

I once learned a very painful lesson. After a year and a half on the South Side of Chicago I visited one of my church members in the hospital. She had terminal cancer. I somehow had not been able to communicate to her that I cared, that I wanted a ministry in her life which related not only to her spirit but to her body and mind as well. I remember in those early days I used to "float like a butterfly and sting like a bee." I seemed to be all over the place. One evening I went bouncing into her hospital room and she was dying. She really wasn't in the mood for me. She felt I wanted to minister to her spirit when it was her body that ached. As I approached her she bolted upright, cursed me bitterly, rolled over and died. I cried for a week. I've never gotten over it. I went straight home and typed out the outline for my master's thesis, entitled "An Evangelical Approach to Social Action Involving the Work of the Holy Spirit." The thesis was this: God equips Spirit-filled Christians for ministry to

93

the whole man—body, mind, and spirit. Yet, too many fall far too short. Someone once asked a friend of mine if he could get more Holy Spirit. My friend replied, "No! you've got all you're going to get because you've got all you want." An equally appropriate reply might have been: "You've got all you're going to get because you've got all you need to complete the miserable little bits of ministry that you endeavor to cast in the direction of God." Again, if you want more Holy Spirit, his fruit, his gifts, find ways of giving or putting to work what you already have. Find ways of serving others, physically, emotionally, and spiritually.

I believe that truly spiritual men serve others and that their spirituality is a direct result of their willingness to serve. Serving, however, is not always easy. It must always begin with the immediate need, whether physical, emotional, or spiritual. "If a brother or sister is ill-clad and in lack of daily food, and one of you says to them, 'Go in peace, be warmed and filled,' without giving them the things needed for the body, what does it profit?" (James 2:15-16.)

History is filled with examples of those who served the whole man. In Acts 6, we find that Stephen, full of the Holy Spirit, was appointed to serve. The first-century church held all things in common. There's a phrase for that—"communism, Christian style"—but don't let it frighten you. This was a *voluntary* kind of communism in which each brought his goods to be distributed by the deacon in charge. Stephen was a deacon, and since some of the Greek-speaking Jewish widows were apparently being neglected in the distribution of goods he was appointed to put this right.

In Acts 9, Dorcas is singled out for her good works and acts of charity. In Romans 16, Paul commends Phoebe for helping her poorer brethren. Paul, in Galatians 2:9-10, is commissioned by Peter, James, and John to preach the gospel but also to remember the poor, "which very thing I was eager to do." Paul never forgot his obligation to the poor. In I Corinthians 16:1-4, Paul is seen collecting and delivering funds to meet the needs of the Jewish Christians in Jerusalem even at the expense of his own arrest and eventually his execution. (Cf. II Corinthians, 8 and 9.)

In the second century, Justin Martyr was forever calling Christians to devote their goods to the use of those in need, lest they be consumed by them. Augustine (354–430), Anselm (1033–1109), and especially Francis of Assisi (1182–1226), all demonstrate a balance between faith and good works. While the church was growing wealthy and powerful, these men were taking vows of poverty, renouncing all that they had in an effort to serve others.

Following the Reformation the great but little known mystics such as Gregory Lopez (1542–1596) and the Marquis de Renty exhibited tremendous challenge through a mysticism of service. De Renty we've already mentioned, but Gregory Lopez is still another example of a truly spiritual man who gave his life to the service of others. Lopez, although born in Madrid, at an early age traveled to Mexico where he spent the rest of his life among the Indians. Truly a Spirit-filled man, historians tell us that the love of God motivated his every action.

I've already mentioned that mystics such as this greatly influenced the life of John Wesley. Wesley was himself a man deeply spiritual whose faith manifested itself in the service of reconciliation. Although fairly wealthy, Wesley kept only enough for bare necessities. He stood five feet, two inches tall, and weighed one hundred and twenty-two pounds for the last fifty years of his life. He never wore a wig, and he mended his own shirts. He once received communication from the tax collector, who claimed that he was not paying enough property tax. Wesley replied: "Sir, I have two silver spoons here in London and two in Bristol. That is all I have at present; and I shall not buy any more while so many men around me want bread." Wesley gave to the poor every penny he could spare. The most outstanding mark of those in the Holy Club—so noted for their ministry to those in need, whether they were praying, teaching, or visiting the imprisoned—was service.

For two years I studied at the New Room in Bristol, England. The Evangelical Revival began on April 2, 1739, and a month and three days later the cornerstone for this first Methodist chapel was laid. It still stands virtually unchanged. As you walk in the front door you see the raised pulpit in front of you, surrounded by a rail. This rail was not simply for decoration. The New Room was located less than a mile from Black Boy Hill in Bristol. Black Boy Hill was one corner of the Triangle Trade (molasses for sugar for slaves), and almost all the slaves sold in America were brought through Bristol and auctioned from Black Boy Hill. When Wesley, young William Wilberforce, and others spoke out against slavery many of the crowd would storm the pulpit. This rail gave Wesley and others just enough time to escape.

Wesley was constantly encouraging social and economic service projects for the unemployed, the aged, and the illiterate.

The nineteenth century also had its deeply spiritual men who were committed to the service of others. Timothy Smith's book *Revivalism and Social Reform* makes the point, and I think convincingly, that the social gospel came as an outgrowth of, not a reaction against, revivalism. The only people in the 1840s saying anything against poverty, slavery, and greed were the revivalists, deeply spiritual men who were also committed to the service of others. Through their quest for personal holiness, they geared the ancient creeds to the drive-shaft of social reform. Smith says that the great American dream—"equalitarian, perfectionist optimism"—comes more from John Wesley, George Whitefield, and Samuel Hopkins than from Ben Franklin or Jean Jacques Rousseau.[1]

Who can forget the influence of Walter Rauschenbusch, the father of the social gospel? The analogy of wealth, capital, and barnyard manure has stayed with many a young pastor long beyond seminary days. Too great a concentration of manure not only smells wretched

[1] Timothy L. Smith, *Revivalism and Social Reform* (Nashville: Abingdon Press, 1957), pp. 8-9.

and is unsightly but smothers and kills all the growth and vegetation beneath it. The same pile, however, if spread around, can produce a marvelous crop. Mark 10:21 makes the same point more delicately. The rich young ruler has too much concentrated wealth. Jesus tells him to sell all that he has, give to the poor, and follow him.

When will the church ever learn balance? In a technological world where many have lost much of the impact of their witness for Christ by failing to recognize man as a social creature, how might one best serve a God of infinite love? Likewise, in an increasingly sin-sick world where many have lost sight of the real thrust of the gospel to change men's lives by failing to see man as an individual in need of a personal knowledge of Jesus Christ, how might one serve a God of infinite mercy?

Must one always find himself swinging helplessly at the end of a pendulum, pausing only for a moment at the extremities of the well worn arc? Must Christians always find themselves standing hypnotized before this monstrous pendulum watching it swing back and forth, back and forth? Certainly there is some basis for a genuine synthesis involving both a concern for individual salvation and social righteousness.

Too many have been hopelessly duped by the words of the old gospel favorite: "This world is not my home, I am just a passing through, my treasures are laid up somewhere beyond the blue; the angels beckon me from heaven's open door, and I can't feel at home in this world anymore." Must our orientation be only otherworldliness?

On the other hand, the church's orientation does not have to be only a this-worldliness. Have not Spirit-filled Christians been equipped for social thrust? Our social emphasis does not have to be an emphasis without Christ, without the responsibility of personal morals to guide social morality, or without the Holy Spirit.

Leslie Davidson's little book *Pathway to Power* states that those concerned mostly with social gospel cannot criticize pietism for its emphasis upon personal religion. The opposite of personal is not social but impersonal. The social gospel does not bypass the personal, it harnesses it and rides it to the stars. Yet, when will we harness the Holy Spirit in us to service *big enough* to require *more?* When will we stop being the priest and Levite bypassing suffering humanity on some Jericho road? The church today, like no other time in history, is under close examination. People are asking questions, embarrassing questions—What is your justification for existence? What have you got to offer me? Why should I listen to you?—and looking for the consistency of her witness. Unfortunately, much of Christianity is impervious to such questioning and is only slightly annoyed. Much of Christianity, however, is rightfully ashamed of its failure to bear effective witness. Today, if someone were to ask, "Can anything good come out of Nazareth?" many would dare not even reply, "Come and see." The church is being called to a ministry to the whole man, and its failure to pull it off is a painful self-indictment.

All that the church does individually and corporately is

a part of its witness. Not only does the Holy Spirit equip her for total ministry, the ministry itself serves as a sign of her consecration. Again, the church is saved not *by* service but *for* service.

The Holy Spirit in the service of reconciliation creates church-in-community, community that loves and cares. Too much of the world, when it thinks of fellowship, thinks not of the church but of a cocktail party, some local tavern, the union hall, or the neighborhood lodge. Yet, the church has been empowered by the Holy Spirit to be community and to serve. The Spirit-filled Christian is grieved by poverty, hunger, discrimination, and the like because the Spirit-filled Christian is ruled by love for God and one's brother.

Spirit-filled Christians should feel uncomfortable when they've eaten too much because too many are starving. They should feel uncomfortable when they dress too well because too many are naked. Not that we should feel guilty for God's blessings. We just need to be careful not to ask God for more than what we need. If we ask God only for that which we need, and if out of his goodness he gives us more than we need, then that's not cause for guilt; that's cause for rejoicing, cause for giving. The point is, God expects us to give, and giving is serving, and serving in the spirit of love is what the Spirit-filled life is all about. Giving (whether it is "all that we have" or the "widow's mite") in a very real sense is getting "good measure, pressed down, shaken together, running over . . . for the measure you give will be the measure you get back."

10/9/74

100

Chapter VIII
Kiss 'em Before You Wash 'em: The Holy Spirit in the Service of Reconciliation in the Community

I once heard an evangelist tell the story of a group of dirty, indigent children craving affection, hugging and kissing anything that wiggled. Just as they approached the evangelist at the close of the service someone was heard to say, "But they're so dirty, let's wash 'em before we kiss 'em." With Jesus Christ as our supreme example, as Spirit-filled Christians we begin by loving and kissing (if it takes that to communicate love) *where people are,* meeting the needs that presently haunt them. The Holy Spirit in the service of reconciliation in the community makes us *sensitive* to such needs. If a man is starving, you feed him first. If a man is naked, you clothe him first. If kids need kissin' and huggin', you kiss 'em and hug 'em first. As Christians we scratch people where

101

they itch. We try to answer questions that are actually being asked. I'm sick to death of the church answering questions that have never been asked. If someone comes into my office asking how he might find God, I tell him as best I can. If he's hungry, I feed him as best I can. If he's naked, I clothe him as best I can. The point is, we meet the needs that are now at his throat; then and only then do we move into the other areas of the Spirit's ministry.

In this chapter, therefore, we want to talk about the Holy Spirit in the service of reconciliation in the community. That means the community where you now live, not someone else's community but *your* community.

So how do we do it? First of all, we get sensitive to the needs of others. The Holy Spirit is the Divine Sensitizer. He gets our antennae up. Someone has said that Jesus never went out of his way to help anyone. If that is true, it is simply because he never had time. He was so sensitive to the needs before him that it was all he could do to minister to those directly in his path. I remember in John 9 where he has just been threatened by the Jews. As they take up stones to kill him, he slips out of the temple and on his way he sees a man born blind and stops to heal him. I honestly feel that if we were just more sensitive to needs we would not have to run all over the countryside picking and choosing ministry as if this were somehow the will of God. Why not become more sensitive through the gift of the Holy Spirit to the needs before us? We could stop chasing the will of God and begin to live it, quietly, effectively, and in God's strength, not our own.

Many of us don't need to talk about changing vocations to increase our ministry. We simply need to become more sensitive to people hurting all around us. This is the Holy Spirit in the service of reconciliation in the community, in *our* community.

As Spirit-filled Christians, we do what we do because we believe we can best serve God in a particular place doing a particular job. "Blooming where you're planted" is more than a cliché. You have undoubtedly come into direct contact with several persons in your community this week who feel discrimination or rejection or loneliness or depression. In the last few days I've counseled a Mexican-American who feels discrimination because of race; with a street Christian who feels rejection because of dress and appearance; with an elderly woman who is lonely because she feels that no one cares; with a young father of four who is depressed because he cannot find work. I've seen people hungry and cold amidst frightening poverty. This was in *my* community; what about your community? Suffering can be so subtle, its colors can blend so easily into the environment that we never see it.

Mike Harrington's *Other American* describes poverty, for example, as a disease attacking at least fifty million Americans. Yet, the irony of it is, we rarely see them. Oh, how elusive they are, God's suffering humanity. Let me illustrate.

While living on the South Side of Chicago, the church I served was on one corner and tenement houses on the other three corners. Yet, we saw poverty not across the street, but always somewhere else. Doesn't that just blow your mind? I used to travel and speak and had no problem arousing sympathy for my own cause but could not, for the life of me, enable people to see poverty in their own communities. How elusive the poverty-stricken are! We Christians rarely see them. We just are not sensitive! We do not have our antennae up.

People in your community have needs. The Holy Spirit can make you sensitive to these needs. The Holy Spirit in the service of reconciliation, however, not only makes us sensitive; *we get involved*. All right, the question now is, How do we get involved? How do we understand these needs? How do we meet these needs?

We have already suggested that man's basic need is to be reconciled with God. If we don't eventually reach him there, we have given him a rope of sand. Who wants a world full of well-fed, well-clothed, well-educated people lost to God and themselves? We can't always begin with the basic need, however. It has already been established that Holy Spirit–filled Christians begin with the immediate need. Since we have already talked about sensitivity let's move on to the importance of understanding immediate need.

Let's talk about *understanding* poverty, for example. Why are the poor, poor? It is incredible to me how white Anglo-Saxon Protestants think they are self-made persons. What total rubbish! We think the poor are somehow poor because they simply haven't taken advantage of life's situation. I pray to God you are not that stupid because it's just not true! White Anglo-Saxon

Protestants—self-made persons indeed! We think we earn our prosperity, even our spirituality. We have somehow bypassed the grace of God right to the throne of glory where we just sit and enjoy ourselves while the world goes to hell, while the hungry are still hungry, and while the naked are still naked, while the sick and imprisoned still go unvisited. Rest assured, God will hold us accountable. Is that too strong? I'm not writing just to the wealthy. You don't have to be wealthy to work in the service of reconciliation. Jesus loved the widow's mite. You don't have to be wealthy to give. You have to be willing to give. Let me remind you that there might be good reasons for success but there are also some pretty good reasons for failure as well. The poor get poorer not because they lack initiative but largely because of circumstances.

Some of the poor suffer from *genuine* misfortune. One Sunday morning I baptized a mother and her five children, and the next Sunday I buried the mother. Her husband had shot her, and my wife and I were legal guardians for five kids during our last year in Chicago.

Another reason that the poor are poor is that poverty becomes a way of life. We get conditioned by it. I know people who are third, fourth, and fifth generation welfare recipients. Friends, if your grandparents were on welfare and if your parents were on welfare, chances are you will be on welfare—not because you're lazy but because that's the way of life.

Still another reason for poverty is hard-core materialism. The mass media teach us that things alone count, that we have to have such-and-such an item merely to exist. Some of the most materialistic-minded people in the world are the poverty-stricken because they are so easily led to believe that they must have things. Frustration sets in and eventually despair when things are not obtainable. Thus the poor frequently withdraw, or play the long shot—the sweepstakes, the horse races (in some parts of the country you can play the horses in the supermarkets). These long shots breed more despair.

Still other causes of poverty are fear, ignorance, and superstition. There was a lady who lived in our community on the South Side of Chicago which was seven minutes from the beautiful Loop. She had been there twice in twenty years. The church, and by the church I mean *you,* can re-educate vocationally and spiritually. Be careful of "spiritually," however. J. Edward Carothers' book *Keepers of the Poor* makes the point that we are not so much our poor brother's keeper, as we sometimes keep him poor by keeping him spiritual. He still feels the pain of his emptiness, rats still bite his babies; yet he now feels that all this is somehow the will of God. I abhor the words of Browning: "Leave now for dogs and apes, man has forever." Man may have forever, but you can well believe that he lives *this life* in the now.

Before leaving the discussion on understanding needs, let me mention an area that should serve as a preface for our discussion on meeting needs. Closely related to understanding is realizing that we can never *stoop* to minister. Let me illustrate.

There was an alcoholic in one of the churches I served. I felt that his life had been changed. He went calling with me almost every day for two months. Eventually, however, he began to fall away and finally went back to the bottle. Several months later I felt called to visit this man and his wife. When I went to the house the door was ajar and I walked in. Through a doorway on the left I could see the man and his wife passed out on the bed and on the floor almost ankle deep were beer cans and liquor bottles. Suddenly I had a thought. Since I was such a nice guy I could have a few friends over and we could clean up the house. I did just that. I left him a note. I wrote on the note: ''Because we love you!'' Would you believe it, I even signed it. A couple of days later was Pentecost Sunday. I had just written the finest sermon of my career, or so I thought. I felt that since my friend and his wife had now undoubtedly read my note and were realizing what a nice guy I was, they would be more than ready to hear my sermon. I drove by their home just before church, went roaring in like a lion, and two minutes later left like a lamb. I have never been called so many names in my life. It was all I could to to preach that morning. What did I do wrong? I stooped to minister.

Pride is no small thing with the poor. You don't stoop to help them, believe me you don't. You look at them eyeball to eyeball. Again, pride, whether it's the best fighter, the best pool hawk, or the best penny pitcher is no small thing. When I walk into a prison, I simply say, ''I was in trouble once and someone helped me out, and I would like to think that if I were in your shoes and you

107

were in mine you would want to do the same thing for me."

It's extremely difficult for you to touch my world unless you hurt where I hurt. Christians who are always attempting to stoop or display an air of complete success don't help me very much. When will we learn from the Apostle Paul to minister out of weakness as well as out of strength: "My grace is sufficient for you, for my power is made perfect in weakness" (II Corinthians 12:9). It's Christians who hurt where I hurt, who fight some of the battles that I fight, who really help me. Keith Miller's book *The Becomers* describes a counseling session in which Keith had to admit to one of his clients that that same morning he had been struggling with the very problem that the man had come to confess. The man was soon in Keith's arms realizing that here he had met someone who was making it in the Christian life but who was fighting some of the same battles. That's the whole point of the Incarnation (God become flesh). God doesn't have to imagine how we feel, he knows how we feel; he's been here. It's the difference between sympathy and empathy.

My next-door neighbor was burned over 70 percent of his body in the gasoline refinery fire in Dumas, Texas, in 1956. The doctors thought that he would die on at least four occasions; yet he survived. Two years later, a man asked my neighbor to visit his son-in-law who was dying of burns in the hospital. My neighbor quickly agreed and upon entering the man's room, he could see that he was dying. As he approached the bed, however, he could also see that the man had not been burned half as badly as he had been burned. He then looked the man straight in the eye, told him his own story, and said: "You've no right to die; you've not been burned half as badly as I was burned." In fifteen minutes the man was on his feet, and in two weeks he was out of the hospital. That's the incredible value of empathy.

The Holy Spirit in the service of reconciliation not only makes us sensitive and gives us understanding but enables us to *meet* needs as well.

Again, get involved. Meet an immediate need. Feed the hungry, clothe the naked, visit the sick and imprisoned; they're all around you—the poor farms, the welfare offices, the city and county jails.

Fortunately, the church I serve is able to afford a full-time social worker. Our social worker, along with the rest of the staff, finds approximately one hundred fifty to two hundred jobs a year. We have our own collection agency for food, clothing, and furniture. All this is placed in what we affectionately call the "Glory Hole." To implement this program we have well over two hundred "Gophers" (those who *go for* things) feeding, clothing, and visiting. If you are in trouble in this city, chances are someone will send you to this church. Although our church is unashamedly charismatic, we want the Holy Spirit to keep us sensitive to people, whatever their needs might be. Sometimes we must provide pots and pans, sometimes food to put in the pans to feed the babies, and do whatever else has to be done. Sometimes we provide gasoline or a place to stay overnight. Recently our social worker sent Gophers to collect a sofa that was being discarded by a family that was moving away. Today I saw more Gophers packing discarded school books to be sent to the migrant workers in the beet fields of Colorado.

We've got to get involved. Not just with those who are on welfare but also with those who are too proud for a handout. Let me name just a few areas where you might consider getting involved: child abuse; suicide prevention; Alcoholics Anonymous; drug abuse; telephone hotlines; local poverty and welfare programs; legal services; mission schools; rehabilitation centers; vocational centers; crash houses (ministry to alienated youth); visiting the handicapped, the aged, the sick; pickup and delivery of used furniture, bedding, etc.; emergency domestic relief for floods, fires, etc.; child day-care centers; detention homes; halfway houses; nursing homes; jails; prisons; hospitals; free clinics. These are just a few of the areas where volunteers are desperately needed in almost every community in America. If you need more specific suggestions consider the Adult Probation Department, Adult Forensic Services, Army Community Centers, Stamps for World Famine Relief, Silver Key (ministry to the elderly), FISH (local food and clothing relief), American Red Cross, Boy Scouts of America, Campfire Girls, Goodwill Industries, Headstart, Planned Parenthood—on and on it goes. Christians, do you want more of the Holy Spirit? Put to work what you already have!

There are people in your community who need your

help desperately, and the New Testament says that if your faith is worth its salt it will manifest itself in service, still another gift of the Holy Spirit (cf. Romans 12:7). My wife and I saw a man on the street last night. He was obviously down and out, ragged and poor, and she's sure that she's seen him in church. Little wonder the Scriptures teach: "Let brotherly love continue. Do not neglect to show hospitality to strangers, for thereby some have entertained angels unawares. Remember those who are in prison, as though in prison with them; and those who are ill-treated, since you also are in the body" (Hebrews 13:1-3). Little wonder there is one commandment for everyone: "You shall love the Lord your God with all your heart, and with all your soul, and with all your mind, and with all your strength, . . . [and] your neighbor as yourself" (Mark 12:30-31).

10/10/74

Chapter IX
**Battleships in Mud Puddles:
The Holy Spirit in the
Service of Reconciliation
in the World at Large**

A couple of teen-agers made a sign for my office that reads: "When you've seen one nuclear war you've seen them all." Just prior to the last presidential election when our involvement in Vietnam was being hotly debated, someone put a sticker on the window of my car: "Stop the war, vote Jesus." For fifteen years now we have been hearing the expression "post-Christian world." This does not say that the Christian faith has run its course; it's just that Christians are now clearly in the minority, and the Western world is no longer even nominally Christian. With war, hunger, and unbelief pressing from all sides, the church is fighting for her very life *and for the life of the world*. She can no longer be content merely to endure the world, she must change the world before she is consumed by some fleeting culture. If ever we needed the power of the Holy Spirit to turn the tide of history, it is *now*. The lines of battle are being drawn. Yet, too many Spirit-filled Christians don't seem to be adequately concerned.

When I see Christians I see mountains of potential. I see battleships; yet too many of these battleships are in mud puddles when they are built for the open seas. Wesley, just before the beginning of the eighteenth-century Evangelical Revival said: "Give me thirty men completely committed to Jesus Christ and I'll give England back to God." The church, perhaps more than ever before, is being called to give this world we live in back to God.

The Holy Spirit puts battleships on the open seas for claiming the world. The tremendous difference between Christianity and so many of the Eastern religions is that the Eastern religions are willing to let the world "go hang." They believe that some evil god created the physical world whereas some benevolent god created the spirit within us (classic dualism). The Judeo-Christian tradition, however, teaches us that the same God who created the physical world also created the Spirit within us. Salvation, therefore, is not withdrawing from the world, it is affirming God's creation through faith in Jesus Christ. God has given us this world not to hinder us but to enjoy. So we claim it by the power of the Holy Spirit.

You ask: "How can I save the world? It's just too big a job." Fortunately there is nothing in the Scriptures against bigness. They continually condemn lukewarmness and hypocrisy, but never bigness. Battleships are created for the open seas.

Harvey Cox's *Secular City* makes the point that modern man is a pragmatist. He is interested in that which produces immediate results, and since Christianity apparently deals only with borderline issues it no longer interests him. Now whether or not Cox is indicting the church is hardly the point. The point is—if the church does not come off the fence with regard to major issues such as *war, famine,* and *calling the world to faith in Jesus Christ,* she's in trouble.

Since the Holy Spirit has equipped us for mountain-moving ministries, let's take a few moments to think big. Really BIG!

What can we do about war? First of all, we can be so sensitive to the kinds of alienation that cause war that we never miss an opportunity for making our position known against war and for peace. We can, by the example of our own lives, expose greed, the lust for power, envy, and false pride. We can go to the ballot box. We can support legislation. We can write letters to our congressmen. We can pray and pray and pray for world peace. How's that for thinking big? Spirit-filled Christians are mountain movers. When is the last time you prayed for peace? It almost seems too big for prayer, doesn't it? Yet, battleships are built for the open seas. We've got to increase our world view. We've got to realize that God can use our lives in effecting real change in the hearts and lives of others around the world.

What can we do about famine? People the world over

are starving while we have plenty; you can believe that! That in itself, however, does not condemn us unless we are unwilling to share; that's where condemnation lies—an unwillingness to share. As I write these words, people in India and the sub-Sahara countries of Mali, Niger, and Chad are dying of hunger; thousands are starving. It's true. At this very moment thousands are starving; not last week, not last month, not last year, not next year, but at this very moment thousands are starving.

Somehow Spirit-filled Christians have to broaden their world view for service, not just seeing service opportunity out there so that we don't have to confront our own, but realizing that the powerful arm of the Holy Spirit reaches around the world. Spirit-filled Christians are involved in a journey toward this kind of world service, beginning with an inward kind of pilgrimage overcoming prejudice and shriveling faith. In the last chapter we talked about white Anglo-Saxon Protestants overcoming the myth of the self-made person which would have us believe that we prosper solely because of ambition and that the poor are poor solely because they lack initiative. The same principle is true for this great country of ours. We have to overcome the myth that America's greatness and prosperity lie solely in her ambition and that the less fortunate countries' misfortunes lie solely in their lack of initiative. That's rubbish! We have what we have not solely because of some particular virtue or gift but also because of some raw circumstances that put us where we are. Try to deny it; you cannot do it.

So the New Testament calls us into the service of sharing. <u>Share</u>, <u>share</u>, <u>share</u>. <u>Not grudgingly—there's no virtue in that—but willingly, cheerfully, for the love of God and man</u>. "All God's children got shoes"—what nonsense! All God's children don't have shoes. Too many who are just as precious and important as we are, are naked and hungry and cold, and the God who would fill us not only with the Holy Spirit, but also with food, would expect us to share.

I know of a place in India where for ten dollars a month you can feed and clothe a child. You can save that child's life for ten lousy bucks a month. The orphanage will even name the child after you. The child will write you letters and call you mama or papa and call your children brother and sister and pray for you, all for saving his or her life, and all for ten dollars a month.

What can we do about famine? We can support the agency of our choice (Red Cross, CARE, UNICEF, CROP, for example), but we can do more than that. We can be looking for opportunities for service. We can stand in the gaps that are separating people from God and from one another and from the kinds of things that would enable them to survive. Holy Spirit–filled lives are willing to sacrifice. So help me, I believe we will be heard with authority to the precise degree that we are willing to lay our lives on the line for others. When our lives are on the line, people will listen. They may think we're nuts, but they'll listen. Stanley Jones was banned from India for his support of the independence movement, but two years later he was able to return. Why? Because in the support of Gandhi his pacifist kind of philosophy had guts and integrity, and people were willing to listen and they remembered.

What can we do about calling the world to faith in Jesus Christ—world evangelism? What do we believe about a man of another faith? Do we have anything to say that he needs to hear? We do if we believe that we have found the source of life through faith in Jesus Christ.

The Holy Spirit equips us for service at the point of both one's immediate and one's greatest (or basic) need. We have already established that if I'm starving and you lay Jesus on me I'm going to turn you off. You lay some food on me, and then you lay Jesus on me. *Don't forget Jesus,* however. If you love me, you'll see me as a whole person, and once you have ministered at the point of my immediate need, then, whether I'm a nominal Christian, a Jew, a Buddhist, or a Hindu, you move on to the point of my greatest need, my alienation from God. I share my faith in Christ with you because I believe he is where life is found. God has given me love enough to want to share this Good News. If you are not a Christian and have found something better than life in Jesus Christ then I pray to God that you would love me enough to share it with me. I share with you not only at the point of your immediate need but also at the point of your greatest need because I love you, because I believe that Jesus Christ is where life is found.

During my last year in college, I found a note on my door saying : ''If you know a dormitory maid so well that you have talked with her about Jesus, would you please come to the hospital; she's dying and has asked to see you." I didn't even know that Flossie was sick. When I got to the hospital I realized that the note had come from the hospital chaplain. Imagine my surprise when he told me that Flossie had told him that after thirty-five years of making beds and sweeping floors in the dormitories at a "Christian" university she had never heard a single boy profess a believing faith in Jesus Christ. To make a long story short, Flossie lived and I learned my lesson. She enforced those words first said to the Apostle Paul: "I have appeared to you for this purpose, to appoint you to serve and bear witness to the things in which you have seen me . . . to open [the peoples'] eyes, that they may turn from darkness to light and from the power of Satan to God, that they may receive forgiveness of sins and a place among those who are sanctified by faith in me" (Acts 26:16-18). Surely we've been redeemed for a purpose to call this world we live in to faith in Jesus Christ.

Again, I can have more fun doing God's thing than the world can doing its own thing. If my faith has not freed me for that kind of living, then, quite frankly, it's not worth talking about. I can go to a party, for example, and not have to sit in a corner and mope as if I'm judging the world for doing its thing. I can jump right in doing God's thing and out-live the world doing its own thing. Not that I'm more spiritual or any better than anyone else, but I honestly believe that life in Jesus Christ is the most exciting kind of living the world has ever known and so many of its resources are still untapped. Again, battle-ships in mud puddles. We have not yet scratched the

118

surface with regard to what's available to us for world evangelism through faith in Jesus Christ.

To complete this chapter, we need to remember that Christ was always feeding and ministering. He still is. He is constantly at work in the world. He is going to change this world one way or the other, with or without us. He loves us so much that he had much rather do it with us. Imagine a world where God did it all by himself. You can thank your lucky stars that I am not God. If I were God this world would be a different place to live in, believe me. I'd rip the heavens wide open and stick my head down through a hole in the clouds and shout people into the kingdom. Such are not the ways of God. He gives our lives meaning and purpose beyond themselves by using us in effecting change in the hearts and lives of others. Wouldn't it be a dull world if God did it all, if he did not allow doctors to be doctors, ministers to be ministers, lawyers to be lawyers, and farmers to be farmers. No, God is determined to use us. He loves us so much that he allows us to be his hands, his feet, his instruments of healing and service and change.

The Holy Spirit, therefore, is going to shove his church into serving the world or Jesus Christ is going to return in all his power and do it himself. I pray to God that our lamps are trimmed. Battleships are built for the open seas. *10/10/74*

119

PART IV

The Holy Spirit in Everyday Life

Chapter X
On Being Happily Though Not Easily Married: Christian Growth in the Home

The partaker of the Holy Spirit realizes that the Spirit-filled life is for real people in a real world. This means that the Holy Spirit concerns himself not only with raising the dead <u>but also with life</u>, normal and routine. Without claiming any degree of comprehensiveness let's allow our minds to turn to the Holy Spirit in everyday life. Take marriage, for example.

We live in a world, in a society, where few people are easily married. There are many who feel that if there are not some pretty drastic changes (especially with regard to the roles played by husband and wife) marriage as an institution is dead. I too believe that many of us need to take a long hard look at what it means to be married, but I also believe that as long as there is a shred of decency left in the world the institution will stand.

Let me add that there is not an obvious text for what I have to say about marriage, at least not without taking time to describe the first-century situation. Since I do not like to build without a sound Bible base I want to take time, not only to share a few Scripture passages, but also to describe marriage in the first century. If this were a sermon my text would be Ephesians 5:21-33, not I Corinthians 7, which seems to be the classic text for so many sermons on marriage. You need to remember that I Corinthians 7 was written at least six years earlier than Ephesians 5. At that earlier time, Paul, believing that the return of Jesus Christ was surely imminent, advises the Corinthians not to marry (I Corinthians 7:38). Time, so he believed, was short, and Paul knew that a lasting marriage took time and effort (I Corinthians 7:34). Paul may have learned this the hard way, since he was surely married (he was a member of the Sanhedrin, and marriage was a requirement for membership), but he never speaks about his wife. I wonder about that. At the time of the Corinthian correspondence, Paul apparently felt that marriage is little better than fornication since one should not marry except to keep from burning (I Corinthians 7:9).

In Ephesians, however, written six years later, Paul seems to be of a different mind. He no longer advises young Christians not to marry, rather he writes about marriage and the demands of love in securing the relationship between husband and wife (Ephesians 5:25). Unfortunately many who read these verses get hung up on the meaning of submissiveness (Ephesians 5:24); so, to keep this in perspective, let's set the stage.

Marriage as an institution in the first century was in

sad shape. Although there was no record of divorce prior to 234 B.C., from that time on it was downhill all the way. By the first century A.D. divorce was not only commonplace, it was epidemic, not only among the Jews but among the Greeks and the Romans as well. The Jews seemed to take their direction regarding divorce from Deuteronomy 24:1: "When a man takes a wife and marries her, if then she finds no favor in his eyes because he has found some indecency in her, and he writes her a bill of divorcement and puts it in her hand and sends her out of his house, and she departs out of his house." Everything obviously turns on the interpretation of *indecency*. As you can imagine, there were various interpretations for this. The well-known Rabbi Shammai, for example, interpreted indecency in terms of adultery, and adultery alone. Hillel, however, another well-known Rabbi, interpreted indecency as anything that displeased. A wife could be divorced for putting too much salt in the potatoes, or for appearing in public bareheaded, or for bad-mouthing her husband's parents, or for brawling or being troublesome or argumentative. Another well-known teacher, Akiba, decided that a woman was indecent if her husband found someone else that he liked better. You might well imagine that most of those in the first century took the latter interpretations.

The Jewish law made matters even worse. Even though the Jewish husband could divorce his wife almost at will, the Jewish wife had no right to divorce at all. The divorce process for the husband was disastrously easy. The Law read: "Let this be from me thy writ of divorce and letter of dismissal and deed of liberation, that thou mayest marry whomsoever man thou wilt.'' All the husband need do was to hand this bill of divorcement, written out by the Rabbi, to his wife in the presence of two witnesses. Little wonder that in the first century, the institution of marriage was in peril. Many Jewish girls refused to marry because the position of the wife was so tenuous and uncertain.

The position of the Greek wife was even worse. In the Greek world prostitution was the accepted norm. Demosthenes implied that the prostitute was for pleasure, the mistress was for daily cohabitation, and the wife was for children. The Greek wife was isolated. She could have no part of public life. She could never be seen on the street or at social occasions. Only her husband could enter her apartment. According to Xenophon she should see, hear, and ask as little as possible. Socrates said: ''Is there anyone to whom you entrust more serious matters or talk less to than your wife?''

Marriage in the Roman world was worse yet. Jerome talks about the woman who was the twenty-first wife to her twenty-third husband. The Roman wife, like the Greek, was expected to run the home and raise the legitimate children, while the husband found his pleasure and companionship somewhere else. This is the setting into which Paul injects Ephesians 5, which says that the marriage relationship must be built upon love, as Christ loved the church. Imagine that! The emphasis is not upon subordination but upon love. It is not the husband's will or the wife's will that rules supreme—*it is the will of*

work and work and work that love might be renewed. Christians get divorces because Christians stop working at the relationship. Jesus Christ cannot save a marriage unless both partners are determined to work. That's what I mean by being happily though not easily married.

What happens when one is no longer able to understand the other's point of view? That's when you get help. I refuse to marry any couple who will not promise God, me, and each other that the moment one feels the need for counseling the other will go with him or her, no questions asked (if they let me down, I promise to haunt them). Work, work, work; but there's more to love than working sacrificially—there must be commitment.

Although divorce is not always a sin, it is always a tragedy. Christians get divorces, but I still firmly believe that divorce should not be an alternative to marriage. The possibility of divorce destroys the tissue of commitment that keeps us working at the relationship. Divorce is like suicide; it slips up on you once it's an alternative. No one gets married anticipating divorce any more than an infant or child upon reaching the age of reason anticipates suicide. What is at first one of a thousand alternatives, if it remains an alternative, soon becomes one in a hundred, then one in ten, then one in one, and the only way out. Love not only works sacrificially and is committed "until death do us part," it is an enabler. .

Christian marriage glorifies God. To glorify God is to see mission in marriage. We believe that God has brought us together for a reason—the marriage and our love for each other enable us more effectively to serve

129

him. We do not exploit each other's weaknesses; we lean on each other's strengths. I used to box. Any boxer knows that you find your opponent's weakness and go to work on him. Too many marriages succumb to this kind of exploitation. The only way we know how to get our way is to find our partner's weakness and go to work. On the other hand, the Holy Spirit, the Divine Sensitizer, would draw us closer to God and to each other.

The Holy Spirit frees us to be ourselves without being swallowed up by some predetermined role. We get bored doing our own thing, but God would have us doing *his* thing in *our own way*. True, women bear children, and the Scriptures seem to suggest that if the husband will take responsibility for making certain that the material, emotional, and spiritual needs of the family are being met, the marriage will be stronger. This does not mean, however, that the wife cannot work outside the home or that the husband cannot do housework. The Holy Spirit assures us of our affirmation in God, and we are therefore free to lean on each other's strengths without being threatened by each other's weaknesses. Again, one can be happily though not easily married where love works sacrificially, is committed, and enables both husband and wife to seek first the kingdom of God.

I love the promises listed in one service of marriage: "Be well assured that if these solemn vows are kept inviolate, as God's Word demands, and if steadfastly you endeavor to do the will of your heavenly Father, God will bless your marriage, will grant you fulfillment in it, and will establish your home in peace."

10/10/74

Chapter XI
Church in a Pancake House: The Holy Spirit in Small Groups

Any church with over thirty members needs small groups, churches within the church. Not cliques, but Christians of like mind who meet together to sing, to pray, and to confess one to another.

The church I am presently serving has many churches. Small churches within a mobile society where people, mostly Christian people, can meet and in a relatively short period of time develop sufficient trust to be able to share and even confess life's experience to the place where healing can take place out of the knowledge of a common bond or need.

I have such a small church or group. I call it my Church in a Pancake House. I meet Monday mornings at eight o'clock with several other men in the community.

Although I coordinate almost fifty other groups, this is where *I* go for help. We have two insurance men, an ex-pilot, two ex-convicts doing some pretty miraculous work in a halfway house here in town, a Presbyterian minister, a bartender, an executive with an internationally known Christian youth organization, an agent from a collection bureau, and me. It's kind of a strange mix, but after some months, we trust one another. I share things with these men that I am unable to share with many of my parishioners. As a result of what's happening in my small church, however, I am finding that if these men can still love me then perhaps some of my parishioners can still love me even if I dare to share with them some of the areas of my life where God is still in the midst of creating the new man. God is giving me the boldness to minister not only out of strength but out of weakness. It's risky, but it's vitally important to minister where people are, not just where they ought to be.

The first-century church grew in the strength of small groups or house churches. James describes their functions so beautifully: "Is any one among you suffering? Let him pray. Is any cheerful? Let him sing praise. Is any among you sick? Let him call for the elders of the church, and let them pray over him, anointing him with oil in the name of the Lord; and the prayer of faith will save the sick man, and the Lord will raise him up; and if he has committed sins, he will be forgiven. Therefore confess your sins to one another, and pray for one another, that you may be healed" (James 5:13-16). Here we have it—churches small enough for basic trust to develop, where Christians gathered to sing, to pray, and to confess.

This was the genius of the eighteenth-century Evangelical Revival. Societies and classes within those societies would meet two to three times a week for singing, for praying, and for confessing. Let's look with a bit more detail into these three areas.

Singing

Unfortunately, most of those around us, while looking for immediate and selfish gratification, are sad and weary and frightened. The Jews, for example, have not had music in the temple since the fall of Jerusalem in A.D. 70. They can only remember a tragedy. Christians, however, should be singing; it's in their blood. I recently read that Pliny, the governor of Bithynia, wrote to the Roman Emperor Trajan in A.D. 111: "This new sect of Christians meet each week to sing praises to Christ as God." A great deal of the momentum for revivals throughout history has been sustained on the crest of a tremendous wave of great new hymns. Who can forget the beautiful image of David dancing before God? "Make a joyful noise to the Lord, all the lands! Serve the Lord with gladness! Come into his presence with singing!" (Psalm 100:1-2.)

Prayer

Small churches or groups also provide a more comfortable atmosphere for praying. I remember when I was first a Christian and I had recently enrolled in a graduate school of theology. When it came my turn to pray in class I would get physically ill. It was just difficult for me to pray in front of others. I have seen Christian after Christian through the experience of a small group learn how to converse with God and with other Christians as well. So many great books have been written on prayer that I hesitate to add much, but do let me say that *prayer persuades God of nothing.* Prayer is people providing God with an avenue or a means of grace for the moving of the power of the Holy Spirit into each of our lives. Again, prayer persuades God of nothing. It is almost like a sprinter poised in the starting blocks waiting for the gun. When the gun goes off, no one tells him to run. In a way God is like that sprinter, always looking for an opportunity, always waiting for the gun to go off. Prayer pulls the trigger, and God races through our lives; it's as simple as that.

Prayer contacts the power of God as we stand before him expecting something to happen. James says that the power of prayer will serve the sick man, and the Lord will raise him up. If he has committed sins, he will be forgiven. The Holy Spirit through the avenue of prayer comforts the dying and ministers to those in need. One night recently the wife of one of our group members died. We were there in the hospital with him, supporting him, loving him. We prayed with him. We also cried.

Confession

I strongly believe that the genius of the small group is confession. It takes time to develop trust. In our mobile society we just don't have that much time. The group has to be small enough to develop trust in a relatively short period of time. Where there is confession there is revival. Again, the classes in the Evangelical Revival met two or three times a week for singing, for praying, and for confessing. I am also convinced that much of the success of the lay witness mission has to do with the dynamics of confession. When I am fifty miles away from home I'm liable to confess everything. There's just something about someone standing in the pulpit confessing a problem or a need. Lay witnesses who would not dare make such confessions in their own churches are suddenly free to tell it like it is.

No one can or should confess to everyone. If you undress in front of Tom, Dick, and Harry you'll get nailed. The genius of a small group is that we find a few *significant* others to whom confession can take place without betrayal, without the loss of confidence. Again, the words of James: "Therefore confess your sins to one another, and pray for one another, that you may be healed" (5:16).

Finally, let me say I hope sincerely that you have a church within a church, a group small enough for the basic kinds of trust to build so you can confess one to another and be held accountable. Small groups are the ideal stage for the moving of the Holy Spirit. Small groups force one to participate, to get involved, to ask the important question. It's difficult to sit in a circle with six to eight people looking at you and not participate. It's difficult to sit and listen to them share things that you really want to share without getting involved. It's difficult to be held accountable week after week without asking the important questions concerning life and one's relation with God. Christians have to know that others fight similar battles. The church I serve has groups in industry; groups for businessmen; groups for single adults over thirty; groups for young marrieds; groups for parents with problem children; groups for couples struggling with marriage communication, love, and self-esteem; groups for mothers of children born with birth defects; groups for the elderly; groups for the lonely; groups for those aching for a place to get involved; groups for Bible study; groups for studying some popular book; groups for prayer; groups for new members, and the list goes on.

Someone has said that the strength of the church can be seen in its groups. Although groups are only a part of the answer, surely the Holy Spirit would want us close enough to touch. Surely the Holy Spirit would have us intimate enough with someone to care. Surely the Holy Spirit would expect Christians to stand shoulder to shoulder against those things that would separate them from God and from one another.

10/10/74

Conclusion

"Partakers" is intended to imply that as long as the Christian keeps growing he can receive all that God has to offer and still have balance, still be a real person. Christians are always on the road, ever moving, ever improvable. The Holy Spirit does not make Christians better than someone else, He makes them better than they were. The ministry of the Holy Spirit through his fruit and more especially his gifts does not have to divide us. Spirit-filled Christians of every size and shape can stand together against anything that would separate them from God and from one another.

As partakers, we allow the Holy Spirit to work through us for the rest of our lives. The Holy Spirit moves us from the righteousness of Jesus Christ attributed to us, through faith in him, to the righteousness of Jesus Christ realized in us—the goal of the Spirit-filled life. So as Christians we have goals clearly in mind but they are never absolute, they are always improvable. We arrive; yet we never arrive. Again, the only way to keep Christians alive is to keep them moving. In short, we persevere!

Several years ago I met a young black school teacher at a retreat. He was articulate. He was angry. He was talented. He was hostile. He was strung out on drugs; yet he was ripe for the gospel. We took long walks. I talked about Jesus, and he griped about "whitey." In a week's time I saw his life slowly change, and the last day he accepted Christ. I remember he said, even after his conversion, "No whitey would want me in his church." I replied, "I want you in mine." I even invited him home with me until he could find a teaching position and a place to live. I remember how relieved I was when he refused, since I did not then know the situation in the church where I had just been appointed. Then it bothered me that I was so relieved. We corresponded for just over a year.

Soon afterward, I received a letter from his aunt. It read in part: "Jim, several months back, got in with the wrong crowd again and got back on drugs. We put him in the hospital and he seemed to be doing all right. In fact, they let him go home on weekends to be with Jeannie and the kids. Last Sunday night after supper Jeannie walked him to the bus for the trip back to the hospital. Eight blocks down the road he got out and went into a barber shop and asked to use the restroom. A half hour later they found him dead, the needle still in his arm. His funeral is tomorrow."[1]

Now let me share parts of another letter. This one from my young Oxford friend, Allan. "So much has been happening. Things have opened up in a truly miraculous way in the school where I teach. The Lord drove me, in spite of my own unwillingness and indeed unhappiness, to do something about starting a Christian Union among the pupils; and it turned out that there was a group of real born-again children just waiting to be formed into a group. We embrace all ages from twelve to seventeen, and the kids' commitment to the Lord is an absolute inspiration to me. Rejoice with me that the Lord has brought me miraculously through two years of misery [Allan, after his conversion, still had to struggle with periodic depression], and taught me so much through his chastening. At last, I really *feel* that I'm a new creation: so much dross has been refined out of me. Praise God that we're captives in Christ's triumphal procession, and can't get out of it even if we want to: and I thank him for the joy which he's given me even as he's given me a deep awareness of the cost of discipleship."

All right! What's the difference? Why Allan and not Jim? That's the issue. For the partaker the Christian faith is a journey, a never-ending adventure with Jesus Christ as Lord of life. How do we relate to God and to one another in such a way that we can hang on for dear life?

As partakers we allow both the fruit and the gifts of the Holy Spirit to assist us along this journey that our "per-

[1] These names have been changed.

fect'' love might become like unto God's perfect love. I frequently get the question, Is there a second blessing? I reply, ''Surely, but not as an isolated experience; there are blessings *ad infinitum*.'' Furthermore, we are *born into* the Spirit as we are born into the flesh, but we then *grow in* the Spirit as we *grow in* the flesh. We are not born twice spiritually any more than we are born twice physically. All Christians are born into the Holy Spirit and then grow *in* the Holy Spirit. To isolate one experience beyond conversion as if it were a second spiritual birth or as the one goal of religion is to invite disaster. For the partaker, Christianity, the whole of it, is a never-ending adventure with blessing upon blessing forever moving us toward the fullness of God—*to finish the work already begun in us*.

The Scriptures talk about unfinished towers and counting the cost. Jesus lived in an age of unfinished towers. Herod was a reckless builder and left many such towers standing unfinished throughout the region. I remember, as a boy, a big hotel that was being built down the street. It was never completed. The story went that it was built without hallways. My how we laughed!

The partaker has the stuff of which towers are made and then completed. ''For we share in Christ, if only we hold our first confidence firm to the end'' (Hebrews 3:14). This is not a benediction, it is a preface. It serves as a point of departure for the stories concerning the children of Israel after Moses, by the power of God, had delivered them from the Egyptian oppressor.

I used to think that if God would just give me a sign to

reveal himself, then I would believe. We don't need signs; we need faith upon faith and grace upon grace. In spite of signs and miracles, the children of Israel grew impatient and God was provoked. For forty years they wandered in the wilderness, and those who would not maintain faith perished. We move therefore toward a greathearted and unquestioning trust in God in order to finish the race and receive the fullness of God's kingdom.

Again, why Allan and not Jim? Why Peter and not Judas? *As partakers we must open our lives day after day to the sustaining influence of the Holy Spirit.*

The partakers see the soul not as a reservoir but as a channel for the moving power of the Holy Spirit. Through this power, we can effect change in our churches, in our communities, and in the world at large. If we want more Holy Spirit we put to work what we already have, that this channel might remain open in ever-increasing effectiveness. Again, God doesn't equip freight trains to pull little red wagons.

The partakers apply the power of the Holy Spirit to everyday life in their homes and through such practical aids as prayer and small groups. Yet, what are the dynamics at work?

I was washing dishes the other day (it's one of the many ways that I work at my marriage), and since I like to get dishes sparkling clean I used too much soap powder. As the suds billowed up, a bottle kept popping to the surface. I would stuff it down, and it would pop up, time and again. Finally, I picked it up and rinsed the suds off

only to realize that the lid was still on it. Then it hit me!
God cannot get His Holy Spirit into a vessel with the lid
still on it. Question: How do you get the lid off? The
New Testament teaches that the lid comes off through
total commitment to Jesus Christ (God, you can have all
of me there is). Next question: What goes in when the lid
comes off? Again, the New Testament teaches that the
Holy Spirit goes in. Next question: What happens when
the Holy Spirit goes in? Romans 5:5 reads: "God's love
has been poured into our hearts through the Holy Spirit
which has been given to us."

Furthermore, Romans 8:15-16 reads: "When we cry,
'Abba! Father!' it is the Spirit himself bearing witness
with our spirit that we are children of God." Amazingly,
we can love as we have never loved before while having
an awareness of God's presence in our lives and in the
world. Final question: How do you keep the lid off?
Surely this is the point of *The Partakers*. Until the
righteousness of Jesus Christ has been realized in us,
we're not "ripe for glory." Paul writes: "I have fought
the good fight, I have finished the race, I have kept the
faith. Henceforth there is laid up for me the crown of
righteousness, which the Lord, the righteous judge, will
award to me on that Day, and not only to me but also to
all who have loved his appearing" (II Timothy 4:7-8).
So we keep praying, we keep reading, we keep learning,
we keep listening, we keep growing, we keep serving,
we keep giving, we keep believing, but most of all we
keep striving until at last we have become the partakers
of the Holy Spirit.

10/11/74